Religious Studies:
Philosophy of Religion, Ethics, Christian Thought

OCR Revision Guides New Spec Year 2

Andrew Capone

Daniella Dunsmore

Peter Baron

Published by Active Education,

First published in 2018

ISBN: 9781980357605

Cartoons used with permission © Becky Dyer

All images © their respective owners

Links, reviews, news and revision materials available on www.peped.org

www.peped.org website allows students and teachers to explore Philosophy of Religion and Ethics through handouts, film clips, presentations, case studies, extracts, games and academic articles.

Pitched just right, and so much more than a text book, here is a place to engage with critical reflection whatever your level. Marked student essays are also posted.

Contents

Nature of God

Background

What is God's nature and character like - and how can we know? God is usually defined by characteristics - positive ones, such as **OMNIPOTENCE** and **BENEVOLENCE** and negative ones such as **IMMORTALITY** and **INVISIBILITY.** The classical descriptions of God's **ATTRIBUTES** have been challenged throughout history, starting with the Greeks; **PLATO** introduced us to **EUTHYPHRO's DILEMMA**, for example. In recent times can a God of **JUSTICE** and **LOVE** really ignore the plight of the starving and the refugee - and theology after the **HOLOCAUST** was never the same again - as **ELIE WEISEL** declared in his book **NIGHT -** Where is God? There he is hanging on a tree. For evil to exist on such a scale it seemed only possible for Weisel to believe that God was himself complicit in doing nothing, or did not exist at all. As a **SYNOPTIC** point, **LIBERATION THEOLOGY** (in the Christian Thought paper) invites us to conceive of God as the **REVOLUTIONARY LIBERATOR** on the side of the poor and oppressed. This new attribute of God led theologians of liberation to be initially suppressed and silenced by the Church.

Key Terms

- **BENEVOLENT** – The belief that God is all loving.

- **ETERNAL** – The belief that God exists not inside time, but outside it. God is a-temporal.

- **EVERLASTING** – On-going within the universe.

- **PREDESTINATION** – the belief that God has already decided what will happen to you.

- **OMNIPOTENCE** – The belief that God is all-powerful

- **OMNISCIENCE** – The belief that God is all-knowing.

- **THEOPHANY** – An event revealing the nature of God

- **TIMELESS** – The belief that God is outside of time.

Structure of Thought

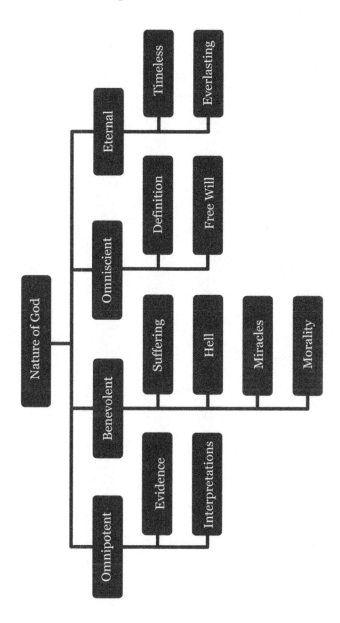

Specification

Omnipotence

- Evidence for the belief that God is eternal
- Interpretations of omniscience

Benevolence

- Human suffering
- The existence of hell
- The existence of miracles
- Morality

Omniscience

- Defining omniscience
- Free Will debate in the light of omniscience

Eternity

- Timeless
- Everlasting

Omnipotence

Evidence for the belief that God is omnipotent

God is shown to be omnipotent most notably within:

- Biblical revelation

- Greek philosophical thought

Biblical Revelation

In **GENESIS** we see a great deal of evidence to suggest that God is **OMNIPOTENT**, in various examples of **THEOPHANY**, e.g. the Creation story, the Flood and the miracles God performs. The Creation story lends to the Judeo-Christian tradition belief that God created the world **EX NIHILO** –from nothing. With only the power of his commands, all things come to be, as in **DIVINE COMMAND THEORY** in Ethics. The story of the Flood shows the consequences when God chooses to remove his sustaining hand. Finally, in the various examples of miracles within the Bible, not least when He stops the sun in the sky to give **JOSHUA** time to defeat the Amorites in the Book of Joshua, show that God can act in the world and does so with great and limitless power.

Greek Philosophical Thought

The Essential **FORM** of Goodness, theorised by **PLATO** in his Republic, was later identified with Plotinus' The One, the God that is responsible for all things. In this way, God can be identified with what Plato took to be the Essential **FORM** of Goodness which gives life to all things, and in this way, God is all powerful as He is the source of all that is. Further, in **ARISTOTLE**'s Metaphysics, we see the nature of the **PRIME MOVER**, that which draws all things to itself, the **TELOS** of the world; the first motion that moves all other things in the universe. Such is the power of God.

Interpretations of Omnipotence

OMNIPOTENCE is the belief that God is all-powerful. This can mean one of three possible things:

    1. God's ability to do anything including the **LOGICALLY IMPOSSIBLE**.

The attitude that God can do the **LOGICALLY POSSIBLE** and **IMPOSSIBLE** appears in the work of the French mathematician Rene **DESCARTES**. God created the universe and so all apparent logic within it is part of that creation including the **AXIOMS** which are the foundation of all rational knowledge. Since it is all part of God's creation, God is above maths and logic and so God cannot be bound by or subject to it. Therefore, if he wished to change it, He has the power to do so. God is not limited by our understanding of what is logically possible.

    2. God's ability to do what is **LOGICALLY POSSIBLE** for God to do.

This attitude is notably held by St Thomas **AQUINAS**. Certain limitations can be placed upon what God can do, including: changing history, sinning, being caught in logical traps, e.g. creating square circles etc. Aquinas's notion of God's omnipotence only took into account what **LOGIC** would permit. Anything that **CONTRADICTS** itself cannot be considered part of God's **OMNIPOTENCE**, e.g. if by square we mean four-sided shape, it is logically contradictory to expect God to create a one-sided four-sided shape. That is a limitation of our own understanding, not of God. If we accept history as events that have happened, we cannot logically expect God to make events that have happened not have happened. That is a limitation on our **UNDERSTANDING**, not God's **POWER**.

3. Omnipotence is a general statement of the Power of God with two possible meanings (**PROPOSITIONAL** & **NON-PROPOSITIONAL**)

Taking the Bible as the primary source of our understanding of God of Judeo-Christian tradition as **OMNIPOTENT**, we can read revelation about omnipotence in one of two ways: **PROPOSITIONALLY** and **NON-PROPOSITIONALLY**. If we read the Bible propositionally we must accept all propositions about God's power as statements of **FACT**. The problem is that statements like 'God held the sun in the sky' give us varied and inexplicable gauges for God's power. If we read the Bible non-propositionally, then statements like 'God made the world in six days' have a **SYMBOLIC** meaning and are reflections of people's understanding about God, not qualifications of what God's **OMNIPOTENCE** means. The problem is that we do not accurately know what it means to call God omnipotent at all.

Benevolence

Human Suffering

Challenge: Why would an all loving God allow human suffering?

Answer: The answer to this is that our suffering does not make God bad. This can be explained through a number of **THEODICIES**, most notably the Augustinian theodicy showing that suffering is a consequence of human **FREE WILL** rather than God's malign will, and **IRENAEUS'** theodicy where human suffering is a part of God's ultimate **PLAN** to help us become more like God, as reflected, for example in the book of **JOB**. However, there is one other way of seeing the existence of suffering by identifying a **NATURALISTIC FALLACY**. Just because something is a certain way, does not make it good or evil. For example, the eighteenth century utilitarian Jeremy **BENTHAM** thought that goodness is tantamount to pleasure and evil to suffering, and could be calculated **EMPIRICALLY** by the Hedonic Calculus. But the description 'I feel pleasure' doesn't entail the conclusion 'pleasure is good'. Therefore, the notion that there is a problem of evil on account of suffering in the world and that this challenges the nature of God as **BENEVOLENT** is a category error. 'God is bad' doesn't follow from 'there is suffering'. Just because people suffer, does not mean God is evil for allowing it.

The Existence of Hell

Challenge: How can a **BENEVOLENT** God allow anyone to go to hell?

Answer: The **ROMAN CATHOLIC** Church encourages the acceptance of belief in Saints who are in heaven, but has never committed itself to stating that anyone is in hell, as only God can judge the **HEART**. Ultimately, God does not want people to go to hell, however, if God is love and if humans have free will, then that love must be all-encompassing, and any human freedom that seeks to reject it must lovingly be accepted. Therefore, God is bound by his own **NATURE** to allow for hell, the place where people send themselves through their own rejection of God's love. Another way of thinking about hell is as C. S. **LEWIS** said: 'the door to hell is locked from the inside'. This means that it is we who **CHOOSE** to condemn ourselves, not God who wishes to condemn us.

SYNOPTIC point - in the Christian Thought paper we consider Calvin's view of evil and hell, which entails **PREDESTINATION** of the saints to heaven and the sinners to hell. Only certain strands of **PROTESTANTISM** believe this: most hold that human **FREE WILL** determines our fate.

The Existence of Miracles

Challenge: How can a **BENEVOLENT** God perform miracles for some and not others?

Answer: This challenge was put forward by Maurice **WILES** who argued that God cannot possibly act in the world as it would be **UNJUST** for God to intercede for the Hebrews in Egypt, but not in Auschwitz.

A response to this requires that we re-evaluate how we readB **REVELATION.** If we read it **PROPOSITIONALLY**, then in fact it appears as though God takes sides and favours some over others and must trust that God knows what He is doing. However, if we read revelation **NON-PROPOSITIONALLY**, then we are more at liberty to interpret miracle events as miraculum or **WONDROUS EVENTS** which may or may not have supernatural explanations even if they do lead to belief in God.

Morality

Challenge: Is God the source of morality?

EUTHYPHRO's dilemma: 'Is the pious pious because the gods love it or do they love it because they are pious?' can be stated more simply as 'is something good because God commands it, or does God command it because it is good?'.

Analysis of the problem: There is a problem with **BOTH** forks of Euthyphro's dilemma:

1. Things are good because God says so: we see this when God issues the **TEN COMMANDMENTS**, when he determines the law that should be obeyed and when he punishes people for disobeying Him. This causes a problem as it shows God to be a moral dictator who, in theory, could change his mind and make something else good. The **ARBITRARINESS** problem exists because some commands in the Bible appear to be **EVIL** eg Joshua is commanded to kill every living thing inclusdng children int eh cities of **AI** and **JERICHO**.

2. God says things are good because they are: this is evident if we think about how the commands of God fit with our understanding of morality through **REASON** and universalisation. This causes a problem as it shows that God merely upholds what is **OBJECTIVELY GOOD** already, therefore, God is not the **SOURCE** of moral goodness, but only an enforcer of goodness.

Answer: Goodness must be a reflection of God's **NATURE**, so God commands what is good because it is his nature and the commandments reflect that nature. If God is pure **ACTUALITY**, as Aristotle suggests, then goodness is fulfilling our **PURPOSE** which is ordained by God. If God is the essence of goodness, as Plato implies, then all our laws and commands that appear in revelation are **SHADOWS** of that nature. They are commanded because they resemble God's nature of goodness.

Omniscience

Definition of Omniscience

God's knowledge can be explained as being either:

- Limited knowledge

- Unlimited knowledge

Limited Knowledge

This position was presented most notably by Richard **SWINBURNE** and means that God is limited as to what He can **LOGICALLY** know. This form of limitation is impacted by the way we define God's **ETERNITY**, but simply put means that God gains knowledge as we gain knowledge. This responds to the problem of **SUFFERING** as God has no **FUTURE KNOWLEDGE** but rather learns as we learn. The difference is that God knows everything we have done, and does not forget. We see evidence of this in **GENESIS** and in **1 SAMUEL** where God learns that Adam and Eve have disobeyed Him, and where God is displeased with David's decisions after they have all taken place. (such as David ensuring **URIAH** husband of **BATHSHEBA** died in battle so that he could marry her).

Unlimited knowledge

This position is the most commonly accepted notion of omniscience and St **AUGUSTINE** and St Thomas **AQUINAS** both hold this position. This is the belief that God has all knowledge, past, present and future. It means that there is nothing that God's **PROVIDENCE** (foreknowledge) cannot know. Any decision is known to God and nothing can fool Him. For **AUGUSTINE**, this position rests on the idea that God is **OUTSIDE** the universe and so his knowledge comes from an **ETERNAL** perspective. For Aquinas this may well rest on his **ARISTOTELEAN** influences. He argues that, since God is not physical and neither is knowledge, God can possess all knowledge, whereas we must learn it.

Free Will

The problem of human free will comes occurs when we consider God's **OMNISCIENCE**. If God is unlimited in his knowledge, and can never be wrong, then He knows all our future actions, making our actions fixed (predetermined) and humans not free. **AUGUSTINE** discusses this when dealing with **PREDESTINATION**; we are predestined insofar as God knows our actions but does not force us to do them. Instead, he preordains our actions and then watches what we do and knows it. Augustine takes it as a given that God does not fix our actions, but does not fully explain the apparent paradox.

SCHLEIERMACHER attempts to resolve the problem by suggesting that God's knowledge is like that of friends, intimate and accurate but not **CONTROLLING**. Luis of **MOLINA** attempted to explain it by suggesting that God knows all possible futures, but Elizabeth **ANSCOMBE** argued that such knowledge would be no knowledge at all. Additionally, Gottfried **LEIBNIZ** argued that this was the best of all possible worlds, so there would be no alternative futures for God to know.

Eternity as Timelessness

BOETHIUS addressed the issue of human free will in book five of his **CONSOLATIONS** of Philosophy as a conversation with **LADY PHILOSOPHY**. He presented the problem that if God knows all future actions and can never be wrong then we cannot have free will. He gives the example of the man watching another man sitting. One places a **NECESSITY** on the other. 'A' must be sitting if 'B' sees 'A' sitting. And 'B' must be watching 'A' sitting if 'A' is actually sitting. So if God sees beforehand what I do, then He necessitates it. Lady Philosophy resolves this problem by identifying God's perspective as one of an **ETERNAL** God outside of time (hence **TIMELESS**).

Lady Philosophy suggested the problem lies in human understanding of **ETERNITY**, rather than the problem of God's **KNOWLEDGE**. Knowledge is dependent not on the subject, but the **KNOWER**. In the same way that an adult can know a phone in a more sophisticated way to a baby, God can know us in a more sophisticated way than we know each other. She presented four spheres of knowledge:

1. Sensory

2. Imaginative

3. Rational

4. Pure Intellectual

A knower of one sphere can know the previous but never the next so we can never know subjects as God knows them. Additionally, Lady Philosophy suggested that God's **ETERNAL** perspective means that He sees every event in history in a **PERFECT PRESENT**, not in temporal sequence but in an **A-TEMPORAL** present. So time does not pass for God, it is static. We experience time, God does not. In this way, God can know all things without influencing them for human beings.

AUGUSTINE discusses the problem of considering a 'time' before God since it was God who created time. Augustine sees God as **TRANSCENDENT**, that is a-temporal and outside of space itself. So God's **ETERNITY** means that God is **TIMELESS**. All questions of God's nature must be considered from a non-spatiotemporal perspective. If God is outside of time, then God cannot change as change requires time. God is **IMMUTABLE** (God does not change), which suggests that God wills from **ETERNITY**. There was never a time when God changed what he wills. E.g. God must have willed the universe eternally.

This position was later reaffirmed by St Thomas **AQUINAS** who was heavily influenced by **BOETHIUS** and Augustine. He repeats Boethius' notion that God sees everything in an **ETERNAL** simultaneous present. Aquinas sees God as the **UNMOVED MOVER**, or uncaused cause. This can only make sense if God is an **ETERNAL TRANSCENDENT** being. From this position, God is timeless.

Anthony **KENNY** criticises Aquinas with his challenge that if his own writings are simultaneous with **ETERNITY** as is Rome's burning under **NERO**, then the writing of Kenny's paper takes place simultaneously as Nero's actions. However, Kenny's is a misunderstanding. God sees all simultaneously, this does not mean that two temporal events are simultaneous with each other. All temporal events follow the course of time, but God observes them simultaneously because of the **UNIQUE NATURE** of God being **TIMELESS** - God 'sees' everything outside of time.

Eternity as Everlasting

This position is presented by Richard **SWINBURNE** as part of his attempt to reconcile God's **OMNISCIENCE** with the problem of evil and suffering and free will. Within the Bible, God is revealed to learn along the same timeline as we do. God learns as we learn. This can only make sense if God is **EVERLASTING** within the universe rather than outside of it. Swinburne argued that for God to know what it is to be in the world in 1995, He needed to be in the world in 1995. This perspective also makes sense in terms of how we build a relationship with God. If God is within the world, then we can pray to God and He can answer. God can perform miracles and take an interest in our lives. If God is **ETERNAL**, then, as **BOETHIUS** suggests, prayers are in vain.

Swinburne's position does have weaknesses. As **AUGUSTINE** suggested, if God created all things then time is one of those things, and God cannot be subject to time. Additionally, this **LIMITS** God considerably as God is now subject to time. It raises questions about how God could create the world if

God is within the boundaries of the world and time.

Confusions to Avoid

1. The Problem of Evil and Suffering is not identical with the issues surrounding the character of God

The problem of evil is indeed a problem raised by each of the characteristics of God: **OMNIPOTENCE, BENEVOLENCE, OMNISCIENCE** and God's **ETERNAL** existence. However, any questions in this section will not be expecting a Problem of Evil essay. Rather, the problems can be raised but should be raised directly with regard to the nature of that characteristic, and solutions should be presented that are in line with addressing that characteristic.

2. A failure to separate and then link Greek and Christian thinkers

The influence of the **GREEKS (PLATO & ARISTOTLE)** can never be understated. They are the foundation of so much philosophy, however, when addressing the nature of God, we need to make it clear we know that the Greeks are discussing God in a more abstract sense, the Essential **FORM** of Goodness, the **PRIME MOVER** whereas Boethius, Augustine and Aquinas are referring specifically to the God of Christianity. So we should never interpret Plato and Aristotle as discussing the nature of the Christian God. They are not. Their concept of God is closer to **DEISM**. We can borrow their ideas to help us, but we are not talking about the same things, and therefore we need to distinguish clearly between them.

Possible Future Exam Questions

1. Critically assess the philosophical problems raised by believing in an omnibenevolent God.

2. Evaluate the philosophical problems raised by the belief that God is eternal.

3. Assess the claim that the universe shows no evidence of the existence of a benevolent God.

4. Critically assess the problems for believers who say that God is omniscient.

5. "Boethius was successful in his argument that God rewards and punishes justly". Discuss.

6. Critically assess the philosophical problems raised by belief that God is omniscient.

Key Quotes

'God said: "Let there be light", and there was light.' – Genesis 1:4

"With God, all things are possible." – Mark 10:27

'Without Him, nothing was made that is made.' – John 1:3

'For God to sin would mean losing control of his actions which is illogical as it would mean he is not be omnipotent.' – St Anselm

'If there was no time before heaven and earth, why do they ask what you did

then? There was no "then", where there was not time.' – Augustine

'Whatever involves a contradiction is not held by omnipotence, for it just cannot possibly make sense of being possible... For a contradiction in terms cannot be a world, for no mind can conceive it.' – St Thomas Aquinas

'God's power can do anything.' – St Thomas Aquinas

'God has knowledge because knowledge is not physical. Though humans gain knowledge through experience using their physical bodies, the knowledge itself is not physical. In this way, the non-physical God can possess knowledge.' – St Thomas Aquinas

'The primary intrinsic difference between time and eternity is that eternity exists as a simultaneous whole and time does not.' – St Thomas Aquinas

'God can do anything, including what might seem impossible.' – Rene Descartes

'I do not think that we should ever say of anything that it cannot be brought about by God.' – Rene Descartes

'A being is Omnipotent if it has every power which is logically possible to possess.' – Anthony Kenny

'You can't say God knows the events of AD 1995 unless it means that he exists in 1995 and knows in 1995 what is happening... .hence I prefer that understanding of God being eternal as his being everlasting rather than as his being timeless.' – Richard Swinburne

Suggested Reading

Anselm, Proslogion Chapter 2 (EXTRACT peped.org)

Augustine, Confessions

Boethius, Consolations of Philosophy, Book 5 (EXTRACT peped.org)

Richard Swinburne, (1977) The Coherence of Theism, p. 221

Richard Swinburne, Providence and the Problem of Evil

Matthew 19:23–26 (EXTRACT peped.org)

Macquarrie, J. (1966) Principles of Christian Theology, SCM Press, Chapter 11

Peter Vardy, The Puzzle of Evil

Peter Vardy, (1999) The Puzzle of God, Harper Collins, Section 4

NB. You will be given credit for referring to any appropriate scholarly views, academic approaches and sources of wisdom and authority.

Classical Religious Language

Background

How can we talk about God without reducing God to a slightly larger-sized human being (**ANTHROPOMORPHISM**)? How can we describe in words an entity that is both invisible and eternal? How can we do justice to the breadth of language used in the BIble for God - **PARABLE, METAPHOR, POETRY, HISTORY, PROVERB**? Is God-talk a special type of speech-act, and if so, what? In this section we range across medieval ideas of **ANALOGY** as posited by **AQUINAS**, and modern theories of language based on **SYMBOL** proposed by **TILLICH**. All of them are about making God-talk meaningful as a special type of language. As a **SYNOPTIC** point, in the Christian Thought paper we meet the **FEMINIST** challenge that the presentation of God is **PATRIARCHAL** - produced by men reinforcing male imagery to justify a relationship of **POWER** over women. How many times in this guide is God described as **HE** or **FATHER**? Is the whole debate set up in masculine terms (eg about the power of God, or God's **TRANSCENDENCE**, rather than **NURTURE** and **IMMANENCE**)?

Key Terms

- **ANALOGY** – Comparing two things, by knowing the one we can understand the other.

- **APOPHATIC WAY** – The Via Negativa.

- **ATTRIBUTION** – The attributes of one reveal the attributes of the other.

- **CATAPHATIC WAY** – The Via Positiva.

- **EQUIVOCAL** – The same word has a different meaning when applied to two things.

- **PROPORTION** – Things are proportionate to their own natures.

- **SIGN** –Arbitrary indicator of something else. Useful as long as we agree on what it means.

- **SYMBOL** – When a term is linked to the subject to which it refers.

- **UNIVOCAL** – A word has the same literal meaning when applied to two things.

- **VIA NEGATIVA** – The belief that the only way to talk about God is with negative language about what God is not.

- **VIA POSITIVA** – The belief that you can talk meaningfully about God with positive language.

Structure of Thought

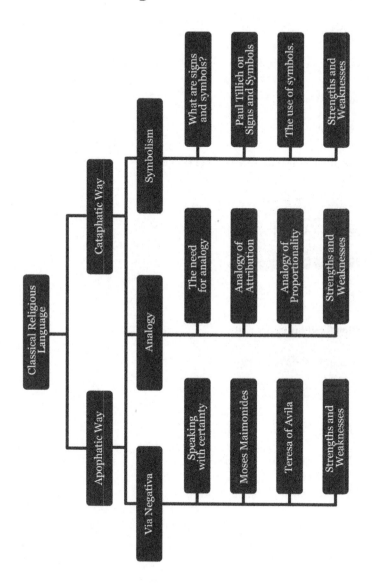

Classical Religious Language

- Cataphatic Way
  - Symbolism
    - What are signs and symbols?
    - Paul Tillich on Signs and Symbols
    - The use of symbols.
    - Strengths and Weaknesses
  - Analogy
    - The need for analogy
    - Analogy of Attribution
    - Analogy of Proportionality
    - Strengths and Weaknesses
- Apophatic Way
  - Via Negativa
    - Speaking with certainty
    - Moses Maimonides
    - Teresa of Avila
    - Strengths and Weaknesses

Specification

The Apophatic Way

- Speaking with certainty

- Moses Maimonides

- Teresa of Avila

- Strengths and Weaknesses of Via Negativa

The Cataphatic Way 1 – Analogy

- The need for analogy

- Analogy of Attribution

- Analogy of Proportionality

- Strengths and Weaknesses

The Cataphatic Way 2 – Symbolism

- What are signs and symbols?

- Paul Tillich on Signs and Symbols

- The use of symbols in scripture and religious language.

- Strengths and weaknesses.

The Apophatic Way

It is impossible to say anything with certainty about God

The **Apophatic Way** is an approach to Religious Language that suggests we can only talk about God using **NEGATIVE** language. Without realising it, we use **VIA NEGATIVA** all the time when discussing God. Terms like immortal (**NOT** mortal), immaterial, immutable, immanent etc. are all **VIA NEGATIVA** terms which emphasise that God is apart from this universe, beyond all human comprehension and understanding.

Plato's Essential **FORM** of Goodness was an **ABSTRACT** notion, not in time or space. And so it is impossible to say anything about it other than that it gives life to all things and is the **SOURCE** of all goodness. But there is nothing to say about it directly. **PLOTINUS**, the Neo Plotinus, identified the Essential **FORM** of Goodness with God, and so God takes on that abstraction.

BOETHIUS, St **AUGUSTINE** and St Thomas **AQUINAS** all argued that God existed in a **TIMELESS** eternity. This being the case, we cannot deny that He exists, as John **HICK** terms it, an **EPISTEMIC** distance from us (a gulf of knowledge and understanding). As shown in the study of Religious Experience, any direct revelation of God is **INEFFABLE** to us. Since our language is rooted in our human experiences and God is beyond all human experiences, no language can adequately describe any aspect of God's nature. Therefore, we cannot ever speak with any certainty about God.

Moses Maimonides

In his work, Guide to the Perplexed, Moses **MAIMONIDES** reminded them that there was no need to ever use **POSITIVE LANGUAGE** to try to glorify God. He argued that two important points:

1. God can better be understood through **NEGATION**.

Moses **MAIMONIDES** gave an interesting example of how negation can accurately lead one to understanding a subject without any recourse to **POSITIVE LANGUAGE**. The example was of a ship and the method of emphasising the superiority of the **VIA NEGATIVA** was to play a form of twenty questions game, where, by process of elimination, a group of enquirers would eventually come to understand that the subject in question – a ship – as it was not a mineral, a solid, a sphere etc.

However, this example is very limited in its use as Brian **DAVIES** commented that the subject could quite easily be a wardrobe as a ship, such was the limited power of the process of elimination. Further, unless the subject is already in the understanding of the audience, the process of elimination will never result in reaching the subject. If God is **OUTSIDE** human experience and all I have to go on is my experience; I will never reach the understanding of God.

7. Any attempt to use positive language would ultimately lead to a loss of **FAITH**.

MAIMONIDES' second point has some merit to it. Consider the notions of Sigmund **FREUD** (obviously Maimonides did not consider Freud as Freud lived 700 years after Maimonides), that we project our **DESIRE** for an eternal father figure to create the idea of God. By using **POSITIVE LANGUAGE** to describe

God, we are using the language of human experience, and in doing so, we are **PROJECTING** our human desires onto an external father-figure. Indirectly, we are reducing God to a human construct and assigning **ANTHROPOMORPHIC** (human-like) characteristics to Him. These characteristics would then be **CONTRADICTORY**. Take for example the quality of **OMNIPOTENCE**. As previously shown, by seeing God's omnipotence as the ability to do anything as we understand it, we fall into problems: what it means, how we deal with suffering etc. In this way, we find ourselves doubting God's existence, all because we used **POSITIVE** language.

Teresa of Avila

TERESA of Avila was a 16th Century Spanish mystic who received many religious experiences and recorded them. In her writings she clearly shows the **INEFFABILITY** of God as revealed to her. Ineffability literally means that something cannot be explained or defined. While not all Teresa of Avila's writings are in the form of **VIA NEGATIVA** (e.g. the description of the angel with the golden lance), we can interpret that she used **FIGURATIVE** language to account for experiences which were in themselves beyond ordinary human experience (e.g. 'he left me aflame with love for God').

Teresa of Avila often describes the ineffability of her experience when she states that she does not in fact see Christ, 'I told him that I did not know how I knew it was the Christ, but that I could not help realising that He was beside me.' This clear lack of clarity in her description shows that the experience is not a **CORPOREAL** or imaginative experience but rather an intellectual one. This denotes that the experience is not ordinary, and that Teresa of Avila has borrowed language from human experience to help mediate its meaning.

The **VIA NEGATIVE** emphasises the ineffability of God's nature. He goes beyond all human powers to understand and describe. The fact that we must resort to **NEGATIVE LANGUAGE** shows that God's nature goes beyond all comprehension.

Strengths and Weaknesses - Via Negativa

Strengths

1. The Via Negativa identifies that God's nature goes beyond the experiences of everyday life. This can be linked back to Plato's description of the Essential **FORM** of Goodness.

2. Since God is at an **EPISTEMIC** distance from us (a gulf of knowledge and understanding), any positive human language fails to accurately describe God.

3. God is essentially other, as Pseudo-**DIONYSIUS** describes.

4. In attempting to positively describe God we will ultimately lose our **FAITH** in God as we reduce Him to a human construct - Moses **MAIMONIDES'** second argument.

Weaknesses

1. As Moses **MAIMONIDES'** example of the ship ironically shows, if God is beyond our understanding, no process of elimination will ever reach Him and so we can learn nothing about God using the Via Negativa.

2. By describing God through **NEGATION**, we are in fact doing little more than refuting any qualities and refusing to qualify anything to Him. This causes the un-falsifiability problems raised by Anthony **FLEW**.

3. We see **POSITIVE LANGUAGE** used to describe God in scripture and within communities of the faithful. In Christianity, God is described as Father. This is a positive description. God is described also as Love and as **SAVIOUR** and **LIBERATOR** from slavery - **SYNOPTIC** point, in the Christian Thought paper we study **LIBERATION THEOLOGY** which adapts the historical events of the **EXODUS**.

4. When we speak about God, we are saying actual things about Him, and building a relationship. We experience this relationship in **PRAYER** and by **EXPERIENCES** of the **NUMINOUS** (events that inspire awe and wonder).

The Cataphatic Way 1 – Analogy

The Need for Analogy

St Thomas **AQUINAS** considered how religious language is actually used by believers as a means to communicate about God and build a relationship with Him. While he began his career as a user of **VIA NEGATIVA**, he finally rejected it famously describing how calling God 'the Living God' we are saying more than 'God is not dead'.

Typically, language is either **UNIVOCAL** or **EQUIVOCAL**. **UNIVOCAL** language is when a term is used in the same way in two different situations: where I say 'the oven is hot' and 'the desert is hot', I mean 'hot' in the same way. Whereas, **EQUIVOCAL** language is the use of the same word but meaning different things, for example, 'I am scared of bats' and 'cricket uses bats'; we mean two different things here. **AQUINAS** suggested that **ANALOGY** was an alternative approach to language where we can use language properly but mean different things due to the nature of that which we are discussing.

Analogy of Attribution

Aquinas said that the relationship between two things was the basis for an **ANALOGY**. He gave the example of the urine and the medicine. If a **DOCTOR** were to prescribe medicine and following its use the patient's urine were to improve, this would indicate that the medicine was working. The qualities of the first (the medicine) lead to the qualities of the second (the urine). In this way, we can attribute the qualities of the second to the first and so we can learn about the first from the second.

This example was supported by Brian **DAVIES** who gave his own example, that of the **BAKER** and the **BREAD**. Where a loaf of bread is tasty, soft and crispy on the outside, we can know that the baker who baked the bread is skilled and proficient. The qualities of the two are different and so when we say 'the bread and the baker are both good' we know that we mean **GOOD** in different ways. However, we know that the good qualities of the bread are one thing and that good qualities of the baker are another. They are linked but quite different.

We can see **ARISTOTLE**'s Influence here where he described how everything has **FOUR CAUSES**, and so if the **TELOS** (purpose) of one is a certain way, it reveals something of the nature of the **EFFICIENT** cause (that which brings about the final purpose).

Analogy of Proportionality

AQUINAS said that all things can be good to their own level. A person is good or bad based on their **CHARITY** and kindness while a dog is good based on his ability to follow instructions. The expectations are different as their **TELOS'** are different. A dog can be good if it does not urinate on your sofa, a husband is good if he does not forget an anniversary. Both are good but to their own degrees. In the same way, when we call a man **JUST** it is because he is fair and deals with people in an **APPROPRIATE** way, but to call God just we mean so much more. We know we cannot limit God to our sense of fairness, and so God may not be fair as we see fairness, but we know that in His **INFINITE** way, God must be just. God is infinitely greater than us, but we can still speak of the areas in which God is good: God's **JUSTICE** and **LOVE**.

We see this emulated in Ian **RAMSEY**'s use of models and qualifiers. We identify the **MODELS** in this world and through our experiences: goodness, justice, love etc. But we accept that the extent to which they qualify differ dramatically. Our goodness is limited to what humans can possibly do, but God's goodness is infinite and so is immeasurable. We know what we are talking about and we accept the limitation of human understanding. But that does not mean that we do not know what are describing.

Again, we see an **ARISTOTELEAN** influence here. The **FINAL CAUSE** (true purpose) of each thing is determined by its nature and so can only be good in its own way. God is infinite with a **TELOS** (purpose) well beyond ours. We can use our language without being able to express the fullness of God's telos.

Strengths and Weaknesses - Analogy

Strengths

1. Analogy allows the use of **POSITIVE LANGUAGE** to make meaningful statements about God.

2. Analogy allows members of religious groups to use religious language to build an understanding of God and build a **RELATIONSHIP** with God.

3. Analogy is used by religious believers and exists within revelation and scripture. For example, **PARABLES** act like analogies: in the parable of the Good Samaritan, the **SAMARITAN** is Jesus, the generous **SAVIOUR**, and in the **PRODIGAL SON**, the Father is like God - mercifully welcoming the errant son. who has wasted his life

Weaknesses

1. William **BLACKSTONE** argued that any analogy must always be translated into **UNIVOCAL** language to make any literal sense. This is an echo of David Hume's challenge to the **TELEOLOGICAL** argument where he challenged the use of analogy, as you can only compare two things that are similar: the world is more like a cabbage than a machine.

2. Stephen **EVANS** argued that there was nothing wrong with accepting that knowledge of God is limited. God is a **MYSTERY**, all we need know is enough so that we can worship him.

3. Rudolph **OTTO** - religious language need only show the mysterium

tremendum et fascinans (**AWESOME MYSTERY**) of God.

The Catophatic Way 2 – Symbolism

What are signs and symbols?

SYMBOLS can be linguistic, pictorial or gestural. Pictorial symbols may be images of the crucifix or a crescent moon; gestural **SYMBOLS** may be kneeling in front of a tabernacle or ritual washing etc. **LINGUISTIC SYMBOLS** are no less common, and in fact they appear throughout language. John **MACQUARRIE** who discusses arbitrary and conventional symbols, where the prior is arbitrarily selected and the latter is involved in an intimate and significant way with the event.

We can see this in religious **SYMBOLS** as a **CROSS** is more than an arbitrarily selected picture; it **PARTICIPATES** in the event of being Christian as Christians are followers of Jesus of Nazareth who was crucified on a cross. Therefore, the wearing of a cross connects the wearer to the **EVENT** of Jesus' crucifixion naming the wearer as a member of that group of believers and holding all the beliefs they share – so the Cross is a **CONVENTIONAL SYMBOL**. However, if a Christian were to become a nun, the wearing of a black and white habit is arbitrary; she could easily wear a blue and red habit.

Paul Tillich on Signs and Symbols

According to Paul **TILLICH**, a **SIGN** is arbitrarily chosen to point to something other than itself. There is some debate here as heavy clouds are a sign of rain. The heavy clouds are not arbitrary, but they are also not selected by humans and so we can accept this as an exception to Tillich's point. A **SYMBOL** is greater than a sign, not only does it point to something else; it indicates that something special is happening. A candle at a tabernacle symbolises the **ETERNAL PRESENCE**, something is happening and we should take notice.

Paul Tillich argued that religious language is **SYMBOLIC** language in the sense that it communicates significant meanings and understanding about God. He described God as "The **GROUND** of Our Being". This means that God was the basis of all that existed and the reason for all that exists; nothing else was of importance - material possessions and ideas cannot replace God. However, since it is impossible for us to comprehend the ground of our being **DIRECTLY** and personally, we do so through **SYMBOLS**. Ideas such as **ATONEMENT**, eternal life and sacrifice and even the life and work of Jesus become **SYMBOLS** to reveal to us this ultimate truth of God.

TILLICH argued that society is what gives and what can take away the meaning of **SYMBOLS**. However, symbols cannot be destroyed; attempts to destroy symbols in a society often have the **OPPOSITE** effect of it becoming more powerful, e.g. the Christian **ICTHUS** was used by Christians in the Roman times. Tillich insisted that the greatest strength of a symbol was that it not only indicated a greater event, it **PARTICIPATED** in the event to which it pointed. Wearing a cross is not just a symbol of the crucifixion; it is a **PARTICIPATION** in the event and an acknowledgement that it was a necessary action. While non-users may recognise the symbol, e.g. the **ICTHUS**, only users will understand them.

The use of Symbols in Scripture and Religious Language

We see symbolic language used throughout scripture and religious tradition:

1. Symbols within scripture

GENESIS

The Creation Stories that appear in **GENESIS 1 & 2** are taken by most Christian traditions, including the Catholic Church, as being **SYMBOLIC**. This is not to mean they are not 'true', but they contain 'symbolic truth'. In **GENESIS 1**, God creates the world in six days. This is symbolic as it gave the Hebrews the seven day week structure against which they built their lives, and enshrined the principle of one rest-day. In **GENESIS 2**, God creates woman from man; this is symbolic as it shows the intimate **DEPENDENCE** of man and woman on each other: God said, 'it is not good for man to be alone" (Genesis 2:18). In fact, the same chapter is the foundation of the belief about the importance of marriage, and how man and woman become "**ONE FLESH**".

PSALMS

The Psalms are 'songs of praise' filled with **SYMBOLIC IMAGERY** for God. In **PSALM 23**, The Lord is called "my **SHEPHERD**". This is not to say that we should look at God as a man who stands in a field following sheep around. But as a **SYMBOLIC** phrase, it means that we should depend on God in the way that sheep depend on the shepherd as **PROVIDER** and **PROTECTOR**. **JEHOVAH-JIRAH** is the Hebrew name for God the **PROVIDER**. The symbol calls us to view the words in a different way. They say that we understand the word **SHEPHERD** to mean what we cannot possibly know first-hand.

1. Symbols within Religious Tradition

LAMB OF GOD

One of Jesus Christ's titles is **LAMB OF GOD**. In ancient Jewish culture, men and women would sacrifice animals at the Temple in order to **ATONE** for their sins. Through the spilling of the **BLOOD** of the lamb, the sins would be washed away. The penitent would be cleansed by the blood of the sacrifice. When Jesus Christ was crucified on the cross, Christians believe Jesus paid for their sins. In this way, Jesus was the sacrificial lamb whose blood washes away sins. So we **SYMBOLICALLY** call Jesus the Lamb of God. As John the Baptist observed 'Behold the Lamb of God who takes away the sins of the world" (**JOHN 1:29**), echoing **ISAIAH 53:7-8** "All we like sheep have gone astray...The Lord has laid on him the sin of us all".

ICTHUS

In Greek, the word for **FISH** is **ICTHUS**. This word is an acronym for the Greek words: Iesous, Christos, Theou, (H)yios and Soter, meaning in English: Jesus Christ, Son of God and Saviour. In early Christian times when Christians were persecuted, it was not safe to announce one's religion, and so drawing the simple image of a **FISH** was a symbol that one believed in Jesus Christ, Son of God and Saviour, identifying them as a Christian to whoever understood that symbol, but protecting them against anyone who did not.

Strengths and Weaknesses - Symbol

Strengths

1. Symbols go beyond language and culture. If pictorial or gestural, they do not need language at all. If they are linguistic, they last beyond the

language themselves, as ideas in our **CULTURE**.

2. Symbols convey ideas about God that cannot be literally expressed. They give rise to **ANALOGICAL** beliefs and present them in linguistic ways that users can understand.

3. Symbols **PARTICIPATE** in what they are referring to and so several ideas and beliefs can be carried by a simple word or phrase.

Weaknesses

1. Symbols can be bastardised into something else, e.g. the **SWASTIKA**. This means that they are not pure in their use. The **UNION JACK** has become at times a symbol of right-wing racists.

2. Symbols can have various meanings and are often the product of a time and place. Therefore, their original meaning may be **LOST** and their value may be reduced. The symbol of God as a **SHEPHERD** (protector and provider) does not have the same value in 21st Century England as it did in 1st Century BC in Israel where it emerged.

3. Symbols are human creations and still do not bridge the **EPISTEMIC** distance (understanding gap) between God and man.

Confusions to Avoid - Religious Language

A question on Classical Religious Language may either ask for an **ANALYSIS** of one particular type of religious language or be OPEN and ask for **COMPARISONS** between different types of religious language. In both cases, students are expected to analyse the named form of religious language and make comparisons with other forms of religious language. However, it is very important to note that student are not supposed to write three separate essays. The primary focus should be on the **FORM** of language specified in the question (eg **ANALOGICAL** or **SYMBOLIC**), and then comparisons should be drawn with the other forms of religious language.

For example, if the question is about **ANALOGY**, (God is like…) students should fully analyse analogy with its strengths and weaknesses, and then compare it against **VIA NEGATIVA**, (God is not mortal..) showing how Via Negativa resolves the problem that analogy has in anthropomorphising God. Conversely, show how **AQUINAS** moved away from Via Negativa as religious language means more than **NEGATION**. The comparisons should be direct. It is a common and avoidable error to write about one type of religious language and then in the next paragraph write about another form utterly independently of the previous paragraphs - showing no connection between the paragraphs and with no link back to the question.

Example Questions

1. To what extent is the Via Negativa the only way to talk about God?

2. Evaluate the claim that analogy can successfully be used to express the human understanding of God.

3. Critically assess the views of Paul Tillich on religious language.

Key Quotes

'In regard to what they express, these words apply literally to God... But as regards the way they express it, they don't apply literally to God; for their manner of expression is appropriate only to creatures.' – St Thomas Aquinas, Selected writings.

'I went at once to my confessor, to tell him about my vision. He asked me in what form I had seen Him. I told him that I had not seen Him at all. Then he asked me how I knew it was Christ. I told him that I did not know how, but that I could not help realising that He was beside me, and that I saw and felt this clearly.' – Teresa of Avila

"God is beyond assertion since he is 'the perfect and unique cause of all things'. He is beyond denial by virtue of his 'pre-eminently simple and absolute nature, free from every limitation, beyond every limitation..' – Brian Davies

'The Conventional symbol has no connection with what it symbolises other than the fact that people have arbitrarily agreed to let it stand for this particular symbolizandum.' – John MacQuarrie

'I do not merely declare that he who affirms attributes of God has not sufficient knowledge concerning the Creator ... but I say that he unconsciously loses his belief in God.' – Moses Maimonides

'A sign points to something by arbitrary convention, but a symbol] participates in that to which it points. Symbols are not arbitrarily instituted...but grow out of the individual or collective unconsciousness.' – Paul Tillich, Dynamics of Faith

'There can be no doubt that any concrete assertion about God must be symbolic, for a concrete assertion is one which uses a part of finite experience in order to say *something about him' – Paul Tillich, Systematic Theology*

'God is beyond assertion since he is 'the perfect and unique cause of all things'. He is beyond denial by virtue of his 'pre-eminently simple and absolute nature, free from every limitation, beyond every limitation.' – Pseudo-Dionysius

Suggested Reading

Moses Maimonides, A Guide to the Perplexed

Paul Tillich, Dynamics of Faith

Paul Tillich, Systemic Theology

Religious Language - Twentieth Century Challenges

Background

Part of the **ENLIGHTENMENT** project was to eliminate the need for **METAPHYSICS,** and for a reliance on belief in God as the source of **CREATION**, and **MORALITY**. At the same time thinkers like **KANT** and **MILL** were challenging **NATURAL LAW** theory as it suggested that morality was part of the **DESIGN** of the world, rather than a product of human **REASON**. Philosophers such as David **HUME** surprised his contemporaries by dying a happy **ATHEIST**. He also sowed the seeds for challenging religious language as **MEANINGLESS**, which was picked up aggressively by the **LOGICAL POSITIVISTS** of the twentieth century. The issue remained - is God-talk meaningful, and if so, how?

Key Terms

- **BLIK** – A statement made from a personal or shared paradigm where only the claimant can decides what is evidence against the assertion.

- **FALSIFICATION** – The truth of falseness of a statement can be tested by empirical observation.

- **GOD-TALK** – Any statements made pertaining to the existence of God.

- **LANGUAGE-GAME** – The belief that language only makes sense within a given context.

- **LOGICAL POSITIVISM** – The belief in Verificationism that truth must have an empirical (factual) foundation.

- **VERIFICATION** - Proving something to be true.

Structure of Thought

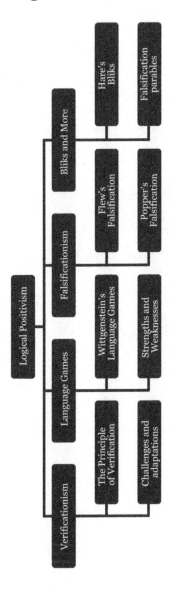

Specification

Verificationism

- The Principle of Verification
- Challenges and adaptations of Verificationism

Language Games

- Wittgenstein's Language Games
- Strengths and Weaknesses

Falsificationism

- Flew's Falsification
- Popper's Falsification

Bliks and Philosophical Parables

- Hare's Bliks
- Falsification Parables

Logical Positivism & Verificationism

The Principle of Verification

The 18th Century thinker David **HUME** argued that there were two areas of human study:

1. Relations of Ideas – **ANALYTIC** statements which are rationally known

2. Matters of fact – **SYNTHETIC** statements which are empirically shown to be either true or false (they have 'truth content')

We see this idea reflected in the 1920's **LOGICAL POSITIVIST** movement of the **VIENNA** Circle, chaired by Moritz **SCHLICK** which postulated that the only statements that have **FACTUAL** meaning are those which can be sense observed or tautologies. Loosely this means **SYNTHETIC** (with **EMPRICAL** truth value) and **ANALYTIC** statements (true by **DEFINITION**) - an argument originating from the Scottish eighteenth century philosopher **DAVID HUME**. The implication of this is that all statements which are not synthetic or analytic are deemed to be factually **MEANINGLESS**. These include statements about **ART, MORALITY** and religion and any form of **GOD-TALK**. This accidentally ended up including statements of history and many statements of science (such as 'the world began with a **BIG BANG**).

The statement finds an immediate problem in its own formation: the only meaningful statements are sense **OBSERVABLE** or **TAUTOLOGIES**. The statement itself (the Verification Principle) is neither sense-observable, nor is it a tautology. Additionally, Richard **SWINBURNE** pointed out that very few statements, even within the world of **SCIENCE**, could be sense-observed. For example, to state 'water boils at 100 degrees Celsius' would require all water in the universe to be boiled, and the statement 'humans are mortal' could never be meaningful as it would require all humans to be killed and then no one would be alive to state it. Swinburne used Carl **HEMPLE**'s example of stating 'Ravens are black'. Without observing **EVERY** raven one cannot declare that statement **TRUE**.

A. J. AYER took it upon himself in Language, Truth and Logic to adapt and make sense of the Principle of **VERIFICATION**, however, he found himself constantly barraged by challenges which show the principle largely unsustainable.

Challenges and Adaptations of Verificationism

AYER presented various versions and adaptations of his Principle of **VERIFICATION**:

1. Strong and weak verification

2. Verification in practice and principle

3. Direct and indirect verification

Strong and weak Verification

STRONG VERIFICATION is verification of something using sense observation here and now. There is clear evidence for it and it can be stated conclusively.

WEAK VERIFICATION is verification though **INDUCTIVE** reasoning. It is probably the case based on past **EVIDENCE** and verification. We do not need to observe it in the strong sense, but if new observations change our ideas then they are taken on board. We find that most   knowledge is **WEAKLY** verified, e.g. that water boils at 100 degrees, that humans are mortal etc.

This form of verification still found criticism and challenge. Richard **SWINBURNE** argued that there are plenty of things that cannot be verified even weakly that are meaningful to discuss, e.g. **HISTORICAL FACTS**. Examples such as theoretical physics, quantum physics etc. cannot be verified even weakly and yet we discuss them as though they have **MEANING**.

Verification in Practice and Principle

Verification in practice is like **STRONG** verification where it can be verified in the here and now and can be seen as conclusive.

Verification in **PRINCIPLE** is the verification where we accept the limitation of what we can practically verify, however, since we know how we would verify something that cannot be weakly verified, we are able to discuss it. For example, even though I cannot see a **QUARK** or quantum strings, I know the theory of how I would be able to verify them and so it is meaningful to discuss it. Furthermore, even though we have no proof of aliens, we know how we would verify them, by visiting all planets etc. Even though it is not practical, it is in principle **POSSIBLE** and so it is verifiable.

However, this led to **HICK**'s challenge. God is verifiable in **PRINCIPLE**. He gave the parable of the two travellers walking on a road. One is convinced that there is a **CELESTIAL CITY** at the end of the road and the other is not. The first argues that eventually they will either arrive at a city or not, at which point they will be able to **VERIFY** or **FALSIFY** the city's existence. In the same way, **ESCHATOLOGICALLY** (at the end of time, eschaton = the last days) we will be able to verify or falsify God's existence. Additionally, I know how I would prove God's existence, with a miracle or a vision etc.; so **GOD-TALK** is meaningful as God can be **VERIFIED** in **PRINCIPLE.**

Direct and Indirect Verification

DIRECT verification considers meaningful any statement that is "itself an **OBSERVATION**-statement, or is such that in conjunction with one or more observation-statements it entails at least one observation-statement." The example Ayer gave was that of **TORRICELLI**'s endeavour to prove the changes in atmospheric pressure by taking a barometer to the top of a mountain and directly verifying that mercury rose.

INDIRECT Verification considers meaningful any statement that, while not being directly verifiable, "in conjunction with certain other premises it entails one or more directly verifiable statements which are not deducible from these other premises alone." Ayer's example was that of **GALILEO**, who proved the changes in atmospheric pressure indirectly by dropping two objects of different weights at a height and showing they landed at the same time. While this did not prove atmospheric pressure directly, it was evidence that reveals it **INDIRECTLY**. The focus here is on evidence. If there is evidence for something, you do not need to verify it directly. There is evidence to suggest it, so it is meaningful to discuss it.

Language Games

Ludwig **WITTGENSTEIN** began his career as a **LOGICAL POSITIVIST** writing in his Tractatus "whereof one cannot speak, thereof one must remain silent", but then changed his way of thinking by the time he wrote his **PHILOSOPHICAL INVESTIGATIONS** having revised his entire approach to philosophy.

Wittgenstein argued that language is not a **RIGID** set of terms or formulae, but rather it **ADAPTS** and grows. It is unique to the people engaging in the language and is meaningful to them. He developed a theory that language was ever growing and adapting and it only makes sense in very specific contexts and as such could not be subject to verification. He gave the example of builders working on a site where they use terms such as 'plank' and 'block'. When the foreman calls the term the workers know what he wants and brings it to him. This dialogue, Wittgenstein argued, was an example of a **PRIMITIVE** language which is unique to builders.

In the same way that chess has its own language and uses of terms, so does football and the two are distinct, therefore, to be 'check-mated' is utterly meaningless in football, as much as being 'off-side' means nothing in chess. The terms are meaningless as meaning is found within **CONTEXT**.

Wittgenstein called the business of using language in its context a **LANGUAGE-GAME**. He argued that the use of language was not private but **PUBLIC** within a community, and each language using community is different, e.g. the community of English speakers, the community of chess players, the community of mathematicians. Language can only make sense when it is used with other members of that language using community, what he called the **FORM** of **LIFE**. In the community of theism, statements such as "God is good" make sense, but statements like "F=MA" mean nothing.

Strengths and weaknesses

Strengths

1. Language Games directly respond to and undermine the challenges of **VERIFICATIONISM**. **LOGICAL POSITIVIST** arguments that meaningful statements must be **VERIFIED** make perfect sense within the context and **LANGUAGE GAME** of scientific **EXPERIMENTS** and maths, but not in the language game of God-talk (a **METAPHYSICAL** language-game).

2. Many forms of language, God-talk, morality, history, art, music, poetry etc. are language games of their own. We all speak **MULTIPLE** language games depending on where we are and what we are doing. We adapt our language to our audiences and one use of language, e.g. Italian, sport, Star Wars terminology, would have no meaning in another, e.g. on a driving test you would not say "the Force is with you", and in an English exam you would not write in Italian. Language is always **CONTEXTUAL**.

Weaknesses

1. In separating different types of talk as different language games the theory removes the link between **GOD-TALK** and what we would consider to be **EMPIRICAL** evidence, where believers do make statements that they mean scientifically, e.g. God created the world, Jesus Christ rose from the dead. In this way, God-Talk is **ONLY PARTLY**

redeemed by calling it a different language-game, as believers would argue that some religious statements are empirical and historical and literal, not contextual **ALONE**. If I can have a **FACT** that something causes me pleasure, can't I also have a **FACT** that I have just had a numinous experience of God?

Falsification - Anthony Flew and Karl Popper

Flew's Falsification

Anthony **FLEW** argued that God-talk was meaningless because it was **UNFALSIFIABLE**. By this, he meant that believers make their claims about God but do not accept any basis by which their claims might be **REFUTED**. By not accepting such refutations, believers make their claims unfalsifiable and so **MEANINGLESS**.

Flew argued that when we make assertions we unconsciously refute the **NEGATION** of that assertion, so if I assert 'my pen is black' I am unconsciously asserting 'my pen is **NOT** red, blue, green or any other colour than black'. This way, I am allowing that if it could be shown that my pen is green, it would **REFUTE** my original assertion. If we do not allow any conditions for the negation, then we are unconsciously omitting any conditions for the assertion itself. If I do not allow that my pen is categorically **NOT** green, then should my pen be revealed to be green, I might deny that my original assertion was false by modifying it to say: 'my pen is black, or green.' Thus my original assertion means nothing.

Flew used John **WISDOM's** parable of the **EXPLORERS** (and the **GARDENER**) to emphasise his point; when two explorers happen on a garden in a forest, one asserts "there is a gardener", but the second shows all evidence to the contrary. However, no evidence will shake the first's resolve and he maintains "there is an intangible, invisible, inaudible gardener". The second declares: "what remains of your original assertion?" Flew maintained that when believers are faced with evidence that **CONTRADICTS** their assertions, like "God loves me", of "God has a plan", they are so vague and void of any refutations of negations, that the assertion "dies a death of a **THOUSAND QUALIFICATIONS**" and becomes "factually **MEANINGLESS**".

Popper's Falsification

The principle of **FALSIFICATION** was first brought to light by Karl **POPPER** in Conjectures and Refutations, where he is responding to what he called **PSEUDO-SCIENCE**, that is astrology and Freudian **PSYCHOLOGY**. He argued that such disciplines masquerade as science but are themselves not actual science as they fail the test of falsification and have no actual scientific basis. As a **SYNOPTIC POINT - FREUD**'S theory of **CONSCIENCE** (Ethics paper) makes assertions which are just hypotheses of the existence in the mind of **EGO**, **ID** and **SUPEREGO**.

POPPER argued that if any claim was to be considered scientific, it must be **IN PRINCIPLE** falsifiable. For example, if one were to claim 'water boils at 100 degrees Celsius', they are claiming that it does not boil at 98, 99, 101, 102 etc. Should it be shown that water boils at 101 degrees Celsius, then it shows the original assertion false, but still scientific as it was subject to **FALSIFICATION**. Science is the process of attempting to disprove assertions. If an assertion has no principle basis for falsification, then it is not scientific. For example: 'your fortune will grow as Mars moves into Pisces' or 'men want to kill their fathers and marry their mothers' (**FREUD**). Such assertions are not scientific as there is no '**IN PRINCIPLE**' basis for falsification.

Popper called this the principle of **DEMARCATION** between what is science and what is pseudo-science. Flew takes this principle and assumes that it demarcates between what is **MEANINGFUL** and meaningless. But this is not present in Popper's original thesis. To assume that **FALSIFICATIONISM** can demarcate between meaningful and meaningless language is to change Popper's original thesis.

Bliks and Philosophical Parables

Hare's Bliks

R. M. HARE responded to **FLEW**'s challenge of **FALSIFICATION** by presenting the concept of **BLIKS**, claims that may well be unfalsifiable but are nonetheless **MEANINGFUL** to us as they influence the way we see the world and live our lives. Hare presented the parable of the **LUNATIC** student who is convinced that his dons (tutors) are out to kill him. Despite how many mild-mannered dons are presented to him by his friends, he maintains that it is a ruse and that they want him dead. Hare admits that the student is a lunatic and that his assertion is indeed **UNFALSIFIABLE**. However, he maintains that it is still meaningful to him. It affects his life, and he alone can control what counts as **EVIDENCE**.

Hare discussed what people really believe and think about things. He gives his own example of being utterly convinced that the steering column in his car works. If he did not believe it, he would not drive. His **BLIK** (unverifiable belief) that the steering column works affects his life as he drives his car. Were he to have any reason to believe that it did not work, he would not drive! Hare argues that we all have **BLIKS** about everything whether or not we have thought about it and we alone are in control of what counts as evidence for or against it. Just as the friends of the student are convinced by the dons' mild manner, the lunatic is not and he alone controls the evidence that may convince him one day.

What we really believe is what forms our **BLIKS**. Blicks determine what evidence you accept. They are shared and life-changing. For Hare, religious language is **MEANINGFUL** as it is about what people believe. In this way, Flew's **FALSIFICATION** does not threaten religious language because unfalsifiable statements can still hold meaning for users and can still be **BLICKS**. As a **SYNOPTIC** point - we can link this to **KANT**'s idea that **CATEGORIES** of the mind determine how we perceive the **PHENOMENAL** world of cause and effect - something we encounter in the Ethics paper.. These **CATEGORIES** filter experience, so that when we hear a bang, for example, we assume something caused it.

Falsification Parables

Parable of the Explorers

John **WISDOM**, who originally wrote the Parable of the Explorers (and the gardener) as a dialectic about the way different people see evidence for God, argued that God cannot be **VERIFIED** or **FALSIFIED** as He is not part of what we traditionally consider scientific.

The Parable of the Partisan and the Stranger

Basil **MITCHELL** wrote the parable of the **PARTISAN** (freedom fighter) in a country occupied by an enemy. He meets a stranger who impresses him greatly and is convinced that the stranger is an ally. When the stranger is seen helping friends the partisan declares "see, he is on our side", and when he is seen helping the enemy, the partisan declares "he must have a reason to behave that way". This is a reflection of how believers **INTERPRET** good and bad events as though God is still good.

Mitchell warned that believers should not allow religious beliefs to be vacuous formulae, but that experience should in fact make a **DIFFERENCE**. For example, if I believe "Thor makes the lightning", what of all the evidence that shows that lightning is a natural phenomenon? Will I deny the evidence to maintain my blind faith? Mitchell argues that we should not do that. In this way, falsification does help to **DEMARCATE** between what is meaningful and what is meaningless, though not to the extent that **FLEW** does.

Toys in the Cupboard

Richard **SWINBURNE** present the idea that we can talk meaningfully about toys in a cupboard that come alive when no-one is watching. While this is not **FASLIFIABLE**, it does not change that it is still meaningful to discuss it. It may be **UNSCIENTIFIC**, but it is not meaningless.

Confusions to Avoid

1. Religious Language is about God-talk, not about the **EXISTENCE** of God. The questions are referring to the meaningfulness and meaninglessness of talking about God, not the existence of God. It would be a mistake to assume that **AYER** and **SCHLICK** are making direct assaults on the existence of God. That said, it could be argued that their attacks on **GOD-TALK** are camouflaged attacks on religion as without language one cannot have a functioning religion. If the language is declared meaningless, then the tenets of faith have no basis. Also they argue that we should be **SILENT** about things we cannot

verify or establish as **ANALYTIC** truth.

Students may want to refer to George Orwell's 1984 where **NEWSPEAK** is created with the sole purpose of diminishing the scope of human thinking in order to control the populace. That is not to say that Schlick and Ayer had such a sinister outlook, but there is certainly reason to hold this view considering the extent that Ayer went to modify the principle of verification to allow for science-talk, history-talk but not God-talk or talk about ethics. As a **SYNOPTIC** point - this section can be studied togther with **META-ETHICS** where **AYER** also features for his attack on **NATURALISM** and **MORAL FACTS** in Ethics. In Christian Thought, the rise of **SECULARISM** is partly about the attempt to exclude **GOD-TALK** from public discussion and force religion into the **PRIVATE** realm. In a **PLURALIST**, multicultural society there are many competing truth-claims in religion and the consensus seems to be to outlaw direct public attacks on religious beliefs.

2. Falsificationism is not primarily a discussion on meaningfulness and meaninglessness of religious language. There is a divide as to whether it can be used at all in a question on whether or not **GOD-TALK** is meaningful. When asked, this question does refer to **VERIFICATIONISM**; however, the reality is that Anthony **FLEW** specifically stated: "Believers will allow nothing to falsify their belief claims. Therefore, God-Talk is meaningless as it is unfalsifiable." So it is clear that he considered religious language to be meaningless on the basis of its inability to be **FALSIFIED**. However, students should be wary that this may not be what the examiner wants to see.

If falsification is going to be used on a question about meaningfulness, it should be done with care, referring to Flew's quote and Popper's original use of the principle of **DEMARCATION**.

Possible Future Questions

1. Critically assess Wittgenstein's belief that language games allow religious statements to have meaning.

2. The Falsification Principle presents no real challenge to religious belief. Discuss

3. Critically assess the claim that religious language is meaningless.

Key Quotes

'If relentlessly pursued, the [theologian] will have to resort to the avoiding action of qualification. And there lies that death by a thousand qualifications, which would, I agree, constitute a failure in faith as well as in logic.' – Anthony Flew

'Believers will allow nothing to falsify their belief claims. Therefore, God-Talk is meaningless as it is unfalsifiable.' – Anthony Flew

'Unfalsifiable statements can be meaningful to the claimant. If an unfalsifiable statement affects the way a person lives and interacts with people, then that statement is not simply meaningless, it has meaning to him/her. It can be called a Blik... Flew makes a mistake by treating religious statements as though they are scientific explanations.' – R. M. Hare

'At the end of the day, if God does exist, then the verification of his existence is verifiable in principle, but if God does not exist, then his existence is not falsifiable.'
– John Hick

'The obsessive concern with the proofs of the existence of God reveals the assumption that in order for religious belief to be intellectually respectable it ought to have a rational justification. That is the misunderstanding. It is like the idea that we are not justified in relying on memory until memory has been proved reliable...'
– Norman Malcolm

'Present-day academic philosophers are far more prone to challenge the credentials of religion than of science, probably for a number of reasons. One may be the illusion that science can justify its own framework. Another may be that, by and large, religion is to university people an alien form or life. They do not participate in it and do not understand what it is all about.' – Normal Malcolm

'Theists do not accept evidence that counts against their beliefs. Believers have to take care that religious beliefs are not just 'vacuous formulae to which experience makes no difference and which makes no difference to life.' – Basil Mitchell

'Falsification is demarcating scientific statements from other kinds of statements.'
– Karl Popper

'The nature of God is totally outside of our traditional methods of scientific enquiry – as a result is God-Talk meaningless?' – John Wisdom

Suggested Reading

A. J. Ayer, Language, Truth and Logic

Antony Flew, Reason and Responsibility

R.M. Hare, Theology Symposium on Theology and Falsification

Karl Popper, Conjectures and Refutations

Ludwig Wittgenstein, Philosophical Investigations, 2. 7. 23. 31.

Swinburne, R. (1993) The Coherence of Theism, Oxford University Press, Part I

Internet Encyclopedia of Philosophy, Religious Language, http://www.iep.utm.edu/rel-lang/

Meta-Ethics

Background

META-ETHICS means "beyond ethics" (metaphysics - beyond physics). Rather than asking how we derive moral principles like "do not kill", meta-ethics asks us to consider what moral statements mean and what the **FOUNDATION** of ethics might be. Here are some of the key issues:

Is there an **OBJECTIVE** principle we can appeal to resolve moral disputes? Or are we inevitably in a world of **RELATIVISM** and **SUBJECTIVISM** where such questions are "up to me"?

When I say "stealing is wrong" am I describing some **FACTS** about the world which we can look at, examine, appeal to, or am I only stating an opinion or expressing a feeling?

Is moral **LANGUAGE** a special type of language where words like "good" and "ought" mean something quite specific and different from other uses of, for example, "good" (**DESCRIPTIVE** meanings, rather than **PRESCRIPTIVE** or action-guiding, moral meanings)? Is the meaning of good in the sentence "that's a good painting" (which applies criteria such as composition, use of colour etc) different from the moral use "good boy!", (praising the child and saying effectively - keep on behaving like that")?

Specification

NATURALISM (the belief that values can be defined in terms of some natural property in the world) and its application to **ABSOLUTISM**

INTUITIONISM (the belief that basic moral truths are indefinable but self-evident) and its application to the term good

EMOTIVISM (the belief that ethical terms evince approval or disapproval) and its application to **RELATIVISM**

Key Terms

- **ANALYTIC** - true by definition "all bachelors are unmarried".

- **SYNTHETIC** - true by observation "John is a bachelor".

- **A PRIORI** - before experience.

- **A POSTERIORI** - after experience.

- **COGNITIVISM** - moral facts can be known objectively as **TRUE** or **FALSE**.

- **NATURALISM** - moral goodness is a feature of the natural world, and so an **A POSTERIORI** fact.

- **NATURALISTIC FALLACY** - you cannot move without supplying a missing **PREMISE** from a descriptive statement such as "kindness causes pleasure" to a moral statement "kindness is good".

Note: **HUME** was himself a father of the utilitarian **NATURALISTS** as he argued that morality derives from the natural feeling of sympathy. He never said "you cannot move from an 'ought' to an 'is'", but only that if we do so, we must provide a missing **PREMISE** with a value-statement in it, such as "pleasure is good as it leads to a happy life". However Hume's theory of language is developed by **AJ AYER** in the theory of **EMOTIVISM** - a non-naturalist theory of how moral language works and Hume never supplied the missing premise himself (but implies that the origin of morality is found in naturalistic sentiments of approval).

Cognitive or Non-Cognitive

COGNITIVISTS believe goodness can be known as an **OBJECTIVE** feature of the world - where "objective" means "out there where it can be analysed, measured, and assessed". So cognitivism says "ethical statements can be proved true or false".

Something about our reason allows us to do this either by making some measurement (for example of happiness as the utilitarians do) or working out a principle **A PRIORI**, before experience, as Kant argues we do in deriving the **CATEGORICAL IMPERATIVE**.

NON-COGNITIVISTS argue there is no objective, factual basis for morality - it is subjective and up to me to determine. Ethical statements don't have **TRUTH VALUE** - they are empirically unprovable. Put another way - **NON-COGNITIVISTS** can say 'there is no such thing as a moral fact" such as the fact of pleasure or pain identified by Utilitarians.

Structure of Thought

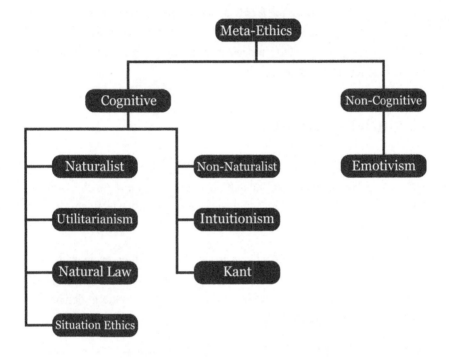

The **NATURALISTS** argue we can resolve this issue empirically (**A POSTERIORI** - from experience) by looking at some observable feature of an action - a fact such as "it causes pain" (a utilitarian concern) or "it fulfils the natural rational purpose of human beings" (the **EUDAIMONIA** or goal of flourishing of **NATURAL LAW**).

NON-NATURALISTS argue either that the truth is a priori (Kant for example, even though he argues for **COGNITIVISM**) or that there are simply no facts which we can identify as moral facts — so that making a moral statement adds nothing to what we already know from a factual basis. This form of **NON-COGNITIVIST** non-naturalism is called **EMOTIVISM**.

The Naturalistic Fallacy

Developing a point made by David Hume, philosophers like GE MOORE have argued that when we move from a description about the real world to a moral statement we make a leap from a naturalistic statement to a PRESCRIPTIVE statement (one with ought in it). This prescription is doing something different. What we often fail to do is explain the missing link between a description and a prescription - and this leap from is to ought is what is known as the NATURALISTIC FALLACY. A.N. Prior (1949) explains the fallacy:

> "Because some quality invariably accompanies the quality of goodness, this quality is identical with goodness. If, for example, it is believed that whatever is pleasant is good, or that whatever is good must be pleasant, or both, it is committing the naturalistic fallacy to infer from this that goodness and pleasantness are the same quality. The naturalistic fallacy is the assumption that because the words 'good' and 'pleasant' necessarily describe the same objects, they must attribute the same quality to them". AN Prior (1949)

MOORE argued that goodness cannot be a **COMPLEX** analysable property of an action. For example a horse can be broken down into animal, mammal, four legs, hairy tail – a **COMPLEX** idea. Because goodness isn't a complex idea, it must be either a **SIMPLE**, indefinable quality or it doesn't refer to anything at all. Since ethics isn't an **ILLUSION**, goodness must consist in a simple **INDEFINABLE QUALITY**, like the colour yellow.

The Open Question

MOORE pointed out that the naturalistic fallacy, of implying that goodness was identical to some specific property such as pleasure, is susceptible to the **OPEN QUESTION** attack. Suppose I say "this ice cream causes me so much pleasure" and then say "ice cream is good!". The open question attack suggests I can always ask the question "it produces pleasure, but nonetheless, is it morally **GOOD**?"

If I can answer "no" to this point then I have proved that goodness is something independent of pleasure.

Moore's Intuitionism

Moore was a non-naturalist **COGNITIVIST** because he believed that goodness could not be defined by its natural properties, but that we know what we mean by good by a special intuition or perception (so **COGNITIVIST**, as goodness can be known as a shared experience).

Moore argues goodness is an **INDEFINABLE PROPERTY** of an action just as the colour yellow is a non-definable property of a lemon - we know what it is and that's the end of it. We can try and reduce yellowness to light waves but that doesn't precisely tell us what yellow is - yellow just is yellow, we know this by intuition. Notice this is a version of non-naturalism as goodness cannot be established as a fact of sense experience, but as a **NON-NATURALISTIC** perception.

Evaluation of Intuitionism

Moral intuitions are said to be like the **ANALYTIC** truths of Mathematics. But moral statements are more than just "true by definition". Peter Singer comments:

"Thus the intuitionists lost the one useful analogy to support the existence of a body of truths known by reason alone".

Intuitionists **CAN'T AGREE** what these moral goods are. So how can they be **SELF-EVIDENT**? Moreover, Moore's theory is also open to his own **OPEN QUESTION** attack on ethical **NATURALISM**: "that may be your intuition (eg genocide is okay), but is it **GOOD**?"

If intuitions are actually **CULTURAL CONSTRUCTS** as Freud suggests, then they cannot be **SELF-EVIDENT**.

Moore is arguing that moral truths are similar to **PLATO**'s ideal forms. John Maynard **KEYNES** once commented that "Moore could not distinguish love, and beauty and truth from the furniture", so enraptured was he by his idealised world of the forms.

Moore also confuses a complex thing (colour) for a simple thing (yellow). Goodness is in fact a **COMPLEX** idea, like **COLOUR** because it includes within it a whole class of principles we might describe as good (like colour includes, red, yellow, green, blue).

Moore has confused a general category (colour, goodness) for a specific quality of that category (yellowness, generosity).

Utilitarian Naturalists

Utilitarians are normative **NATURALISTS** because they argue that goodness is an observable feature of the natural world - part of our **A POSTERIORI** experience of pleasure and pain. So to work out what is good, we need to project into the future and balance the likely pain and pleasure of our choice. That which maximises happiness and minimises pain is good, and actions that do the opposite are bad.

Utilitarians quite openly commit the **NATURALISTIC FALLACY** (which they argue isn't a fallacy at all) arguing that it is obviously good to pursue happiness because that as a matter of fact is the goal that all humans are pursuing. They give a **TELEOLOGICAL** justification for goodness, just as **NATURAL LAW** theorists such as **AQUINAS** follow Aristotle in linking goodness to **HUMAN FLOURISHING**.

The philosopher **JOHN SEARLE** gives us another naturalist way out of the supposed fallacy. If I promise to pay you £500 then I am doing two things - I am agreeing to play the promising game which involves **OBLIGATION** to pay your money back, and I am accepting that part of the rules of the game, fixed by society, in that I can only break this promise if a large, overriding reason appears for doing so (for example, the money is stolen from me and I am bankrupt, so can't pay it back).

So the making of a promise is a **FACT** but because of the logical feature of promising - that I agree to it creates obligations for me - this allows us to move from a descriptive **IS** statement (Brian owes me £5) to a value **OUGHT** statement "you ought to keep your promise".

Ayer's Emotivism ("Expressivism")

A.J. Ayer (1910-1989) formed part of a school of linguistic philosophy called **LOGICAL POSITIVISM** which had at its heart the **VERIFICATION PRINCIPLE**. Truth claims had to be verified true or false by sense-experience. His theory is a theory of **NON-COGNITIVISM** as he argues moral statements add no facts – just opinions which cannot be established true or false empirically. So moral truth cannot be **KNOWN** as objective fact.

> *"The fundamental ethical concepts are unanalysable inasmuch as there is no criterion by which to judge the validity of the judgements. They are mere pseudo-concepts. The presence of an ethical symbol adds nothing to its factual content. Thus if I say to someone 'You acted wrongly in stealing the money,' I am not stating anything more than if I had simply stated 'you stole the money'". Language, Truth and Logic (1971)*

This approach to moral language was a development of **HUME's FORK** - an argument about language developed by David Hume. Hume argued that statements about the real world were of two sorts - they were either analytic or synthetic: either **LOGICAL TRUTHS** or **STATEMENTS OF FACT**.

An analytic statement is true by definition (2 + 2 = 4), a **SYNTHETIC** statement true by experience. So "all bachelors are unmarried" is true by definition, whereas "John is a bachelor" is true by experience (John might be married so that would make the statement **EMPIRICALLY** false). As moral statements are neither **ANALYTIC** (they'd have nothing useful to say about the **REAL** world if they were) or **SYNTHETIC** (not **VERIFIABLE**) they are logically and empirically meaningless.

Ayer put the same point another way.

> "The presence of an ethical symbol in a proposition adds nothing to its factual content". (1971:142).

Ayer believed that problems arose when the **NATURALISTS**, such as the **UTILITARIANS** claimed an empirical basis for goodness in the balance of pleasure over pain. What happens when one person's pleasure is another person's pain? Consider that someone steals your wallet. To you, stealing is wrong because it causes you pain. To the thief, stealing is good, because it gives her money to buy food, and she's starving. Stealing appears to be **BOTH** right and wrong at the same time.

This contradictory result indicates there can be no **FACT** of morality – just an **OPINION**.

> "It is not self-contradictory to say some pleasant things are not good, or that some bad things are desired". (Ayer, 1971:139)

Ayer means by this that if I say "you were wrong to steal" there is no additional **FACT** introduced by the word "wrong" - only an **EXPRESSION** of a feeling of disapproval. Note he argues the word **GOOD** is not describing a feeling but, in is own words "**EVINCING**" a feeling - like letting out a squeal if you hit your thumb, **"OUCH"**!.

"Stealing money is wrong expresses no proposition which can be either true or false. It's as if I had written "stealing money!!!" where the exclamation marks show a special sort of moral disapproval". A.J. Ayer

Evaluation - Ayer

Ayer's view seems to be a radical **SUBJECTIVISM** suggesting morality is just "up to me". It seems to strengthen the case for **RELATIVISM** that makes moral debate impossible and disagreements insoluble, even though this is not a theory of **NORMS** but of **MEANING**.

Ayer's view is based on a **FALLACY**. Ludwig Wittgenstein demonstrated that language is part of a game we play with shared rules. **MORAL** language is neither analytic nor synthetic but rather, **PRESCRIPTIVE** as Hare suggests (below). Ayer has committed a fallacy like saying "the world is either square or flat". It's neither.

According to Alasdair **MACINTYRE** in After Virtue, emotivism obliterates the distinction between manipulative and non-manipulative behaviour. There is no longer such an idea as a **VALID REASON**. Moral discourse is simply about manipulating you to adopt my point of view.

Absolutism & Relativism

Both these are ambiguous ideas. Relativism has three meanings: **PARTICULAR** to culture, **CONSEQUENTIALIST** and **SUBJECTIVE** (up to me).

Absolutism has three meanings which are the opposite: **UNIVERSAL** (applies everywhere and for all time), **NON-CONSEQUENTIALIST** and **OBJECTIVE**.

Theories may not be consistently absolute in all three meanings as the table overleaf demonstrates.

Theory	Universal	Non-consequentialist	Objective
Utilitarianism	YES, it claims we all experience pleasure and pain	NO, as goodness is always relative to maximising happiness	YES, as pleasure and happiness are measurable otherwise they couldn't be maximised
Situation Ethics	YES, as we can all understand and live by agape love	NO, as we maximise the value of love	YES, as there is a measurable test for ethical goodness
Kantian Ethics	YES, as we can all universalise a priori	YES, as categorical absolute rules are created	YES, as the Moral Law exists as an objective truth
Natural Law	YES, as we all share one rational human nature	NO, as secondary precepts are applications of reason and never absolute	YES, the world and human nature is set up in certain way - and operates by objective laws

We may therefore conclude that only **KANTIAN** ethics is absolute in all three possible meanings. The other theories have an **ABSOLUTE** element - they have a non-negotiable principle at their heart. That's why Joseph Fletcher calls his theory ~ **PRINCIPLED RELATIVISM** (the absolute principle is **AGAPE**) made relative always to consequences - the second meaning of relativism given earlier.

Is **EMOTIVISM** a form of **RELATIVISM?** It is a meta-ethical theory, not a normative one, and so in one sense the question is a **CATEGORY MISTAKE** as the term can only be applied to the derivation of norms. However, in stressing the absence of **MORAL FACTS** and arguing that moral statements are neither analytic nor synthetic, and therefore meaningless in empirical terms, emotivism does appear to reinforce **SUBJECTIVISM** (our first meaning of relativism).

C.L. Stevenson's Emotivism

Stevenson argued that three criteria must be fulfilled when we use the word "good":

1. We must be able to agree that the action is good.

2. The action must have a **MAGNETISM** - we must want to do it, and feel an **INTEREST** in its being done.

3. The action cannot be verified empirically by appeal to facts.

So moral language has an **EMOTIVE** meaning and a **PERSUASIVE** meaning – we are encouraging others to share our attitude. This is why we bother to **ARGUE** about ethics, whereas on questions of taste we "agree to differ".

"Good has an emotive meaning...when a person morally approves of something, he experiences a rich feeling of security when it prospers and is indignant or shocked when it doesn't". C.L .Stevenson.

R.M.Hare's Prescriptivism

R.M. Hare (1919-2002) argued that moral judgements have an **EMOTIVE** and a **PRESCRIPTIVE** meaning. This implicitly disagrees with the view of **HUME** and **AYER** who argue that meaningful statements are either analytic (true by definition) or synthetic (true by experience.)

Prescriptions are forms of **IMPERATIVE**: "you oughtn't steal" is equivalent to saying "**DON'T STEAL!**".

Hare agrees that you cannot derive a **PRESCRIPTION** such as "run!" from a description "there's a bull over there!" as there is a **SUBJECTIVE** element (I may choose to walk calmly or stand and wave my red rag). I am free to judge, hence the title of his book **FREEDOM** and **REASON**.

Hare follows **KANT** (even though Hare is a preference utilitarian) in arguing that **REASONABLENESS** lies in the **UNIVERSALISABILITY** of moral statements. Anyone who uses terms like "right" and "ought" are **LOGICALLY COMMITTED** to the idea that any action in relevantly similar circumstances is also wrong (see Kant's first formula of the **CATEGORICAL IMPERATIVE**).

So if Nazis say "Jews must be killed", they must also judge that if, say it turns out that they are of Jewish origin, then they too must be killed. Only a **FANATIC** would say this.

Hare argues for the importance of **MORAL PRINCIPLES** rather than **RULES**. It is like learning to drive a car:

"The good driver is one whose actions are so exactly governed by principles which have become a habit with him, that he normally does not have to think what to do. But all road conditions are various, and

therefore it is unwise to let all one's driving become a matter of habit".
(Hare, Language of Morals, page 63)

Evaluation - Prescriptivism

Hare is still denying there are **OBJECTIVE** moral truths. We are free to choose our own principles and determine our actions according to our desires and preferences – there is no objective right and wrong independent of our choosing, but then having chosen, we must be able to universalise it. As a **NON-NATURALIST** he avoids reference to any final **TELOS** such as human flourishing.

Philippa **FOOT** criticised Hare in her lecture in 1958 ("Moral Beliefs") for allowing terribly immoral acts (and people) to be called "moral" simply because they are **CONSISTENT**. We cannot avoid approving the statement "If I was a murderer, I would want to be dead too if I support the death penalty". Prescriptivism cannot help justifying **FANATICISM**.

In his later book **MORAL THINKING** Hare brings together **PRESCRIPTIVISM** and his version of **PREFERENCE UTILITARIANISM**. To prescribe a moral action is to universalise that action – in universalising

"I must take into account all the ideals and preferences held by all those who will be affected and I cannot give any weight to my own ideals. The ultimate effect of this application of universalisability is that a moral judgement must ultimately be based on the maximum possible satisfaction of the preferences of all those affected by it". (Peter Singer)

Hare's pupil **PETER SINGER** builds on this idea to give prescriptivism an **OBJECTIVE** basis in his own version of preference utilitarianism. We are asked to universalise from a neutral, universal viewpoint.

So in the end prescriptivism escapes the charge of being another form of radical **SUBJECTIVISM**.

The Legacy of David Hume

David Hume argued that morality was a matter of acting on desires and feelings. Moral reasoning really reduces to the question "what do I want?" – it remains radically **SUBJECTIVE**. If Hume is right, there is no answer to the question "why should I be moral?" or "why should I be benevolent?". If I don't want to be moral, that seems to be the end of the argument.

J.L. MACKIE (Inventing Right and Wrong,1977) argues that the common view of moral language implies that there are some objective moral facts in the universe. But this view is a **MISTAKE**. There are no moral facts. We can only base our moral judgements on **FEELINGS** and **DESIRES**.

The **INTUITIONISTS** (G.E. Moore, H.A. Prichard, W.D. Ross) are arguing that there are **MORAL FACTS** but that we can only know them **NON-NATURALLY** as internal intuitions. This seems to be an attempt to have our cake and eat it.

R.M. HARE does have an answer to the question "why should I be moral?" At least in his later book **MORAL THINKING**, Hare argues that people are more likely to be happy if they follow universal **PRESCRIPTIVISM** and reason from a viewpoint that takes into account the interests and preferences of all people affected by my decision. However, this is an appeal to **SELF-INTEREST** – Hare is still an **SUBJECTIVIST**.

NATURAL LAW suggests a **NATURALIST** reason for being moral : we are moral to achieve personal and social **FLOURISHING**. If we can share the insights of psychology and philosophy we can come to a shared (if still **RELATIVISTIC**, cultural) view of what will build the excellent life. Naturalism has undergone a resurgence in the twentieth century, led by Geoffrey **WARNOCK** (1971, The Object of Morality) and Alasdair **MACINTYRE** (1981, After Virtue).

More recent, subtler, attempts to escape **SUBJECTIVISM** are to be found in John **RAWLS'** A Theory of Justice, which asks us to assume the role of an avatar in a space ship, imagining we are in an **ORIGINAL POSITION** heading to a new world where we don't know our gender, intelligence, race, or circumstances. What rules would we formulate for this world? Rawls, like Hare, brings **KANT** back into the forefront of meta-ethical debate.

Key Confusions to Avoid

1. "Utilitarianism is a meta-ethical theory". No, utilitarianism is a **NORMATIVE** theory that is built upon the meta-ethical view that the foundation of morals is **NATURALISTIC** - out there to be observed in the world **A POSTERIORI** (by experience of pleasure and pain). Meta-ethics has nothing to say about exactly how **NORMS** (values of goodness) are derived.

2. "Normative ethics is more useful than meta-ethics". This old exam question has a central ambiguity - more useful for what and to whom? If you're facing a **MORAL DILEMMA**, meta-ethics has no use at all

because it doesn't produce a structure of thought for deciding what to do.

3. "Meta-ethics is boring". This is because it is sometimes badly taught. Actually the structure of morality that builds from meta-ethical **FOUNDATIONS** to **NORMATIVE THEORY** to **PRACTICAL CONCLUSION** is a fascinating one, and we need to think long and hard about how we are to solve moral problems - both **GLOBAL** (war, famine, injustice, poverty, exploitation) and **PERSONAL** (euthanasia, sexual ethics) even though the specification is biased (as in western thought generally) towards the personal.

Possible Future Questions

1. "The meaning of the word 'good' is the defining question in the study of ethics". Discuss

2. Critically consider whether ethical terms such as good, bad, right and wrong have an objective factual basis that makes them true or false.

3. "Ethical statements are merely an expression of an emotion". Discuss

4. Evaluate the view that ethical statements are meaningless.

5. "People know what's right or wrong by a common sense intuition". Discuss

6. Critically contrast the views of intuitionists and emotivists on the origin and meaning of ethical statements.

Key Quotes - Meta-ethics

"That which is meant by "good" is the only simple object of thought which is peculiar to ethics". G.E. Moore

"As this ought expresses some new relation it is necessary that it should be observed and explained and at the same time that a reason be given". David Hume

"The use of "That is bad!" implies an appeal to an objective and impersonal standard in a way in which "I disapprove of this; do so as well!" does not. If emotivism is true, moral language is seriously misleading". Alasdair MacIntyre

"Good serves only as an emotive sign expressing our attitude to something, and perhaps evoking similar attitudes in other persons". A.J. Ayer

"To ask whether I ought to do A in these circumstances is to ask whether or not I will that doing A in these circumstances should become a universal law". R.M. Hare

"We have an idea of good ends that morality serves. Even if we are deontologists, we still think that there is a point to morality, to do with better outcomes – truth-telling generally produces better outcomes than lying. These ends can be put into non-moral language in terms of happiness, flourishing, welfare, or equality". Louis Pojman

Suggested Reading

Moore, G.E. (1903) Principia Ethica, Chapter II (see peped.org/meta-ethics/extract)

Ayer, A.J. (1936) Language, Truth and Logic, London: Victor Gollancz, Chapter 6 (see peped.org/meta-ethics/extract)

Mackie, J.L. (1977) Ethics: Inventing Right and Wrong, London: Penguin Books, Part 1.3

Conscience

Issues

There are four major issues in a study of conscience.

- What is the **ORIGIN** of conscience: does it come from God, our upbringing or from reason?

- What is the relation between **MORALITY** and **GUILT** feelings? Is guilt a product of certain complexes, such as Freud's **OEDIPUS COMPLEX?**

- How does conscience **WORK**: is it a **MENTAL PROCESS** and so part of our **REASON**, a **FEELING**, or a **VOICE** in our heads (e.g. the voice of God?)?

- Can we go against our conscience and choose to reject it, in other words, is conscience **FALLIBLE** and so likely to make mistakes, or is it inerrant (incapable of error)? What is the relationship between conscience and human **WILL**?

Specification

Requires us to consider **FREUD**'s Psychological approach and **AQUINAS'** Theological Approach, to compare and critically evaluate these two theories. We are at liberty to contrast them with Eric **FROMM, BUTLER** or **NEWMAN** or anyone else - the syllabus is open-ended about additional material. We do, however, need to compare and contrast them with philosophers/authors of a different persuasion - so these are included in this guide. Students need to decide which is most relevant to their own approach of critical analysis and evaluation of Aquinas and Freud.

The Psychology of Conscience - Freud

Background

ENLIGHTENMENT – believed in reason and measurement but also hypothesis tested **A POSTERIORI.** Freud shared this belief that science could probe the deepest unconscious recesses of the human mind and so contribute to the advancement of human welfare.

- **COPERNICUS** taught us that humans were not the centre of the universe.

- **DARWIN** taught us that humans were just another species of animal.

- **FREUD** taught us that humans were not rational actors, but rather are driven by unconscious, primitive, instinctual desires.

Key Terms

- **CATEGORICAL IMPERATIVE** unconditional demands of the superego whose violation produces guilt

- **CONSCIENCE** The part of human consciousness that guides moral decisions and equivalent to the superego

- **EGO** The part of the human mind that forms our idea of self and presents a coherent image to the outside world. The ego longs for a moral guide.

- **ID** The part of the human mind which processes passions and emotions. It is non-moral and is often in conflict with ego and superego.

- **SUPEREGO** The part of the human mind which regulates behaviour, formed in childhood by relationships with authority figures (father and mother) and by praise and blame.

- **REPRESSION** The suppression of our real emotions because they do not conform to ego-identity or are categorized as shameful by the superego.

- **EROS** The creative life-force which is also the mischief-maker as it encourages the ego to take risks and cross boundaries.

- **THANATOS** The death-instinct in conflict with eros, which appears in destructive patterns of behaviour (self-harm, aggression, and suicide).

- **UNCONSCIOUS** That part of the iceberg of the human mind which lies unseen but nonetheless influences and even controls behaviour.

- **LIBIDO** The sexual instinct which forms part of eros and is often repressed or overly controlled by the superego.

- **NEUROSIS** Mental illness which results from a failure to create a coherent and harmonious ego. Examples might be hysteria, obsessive-compulsive disorders (e.g. washing rituals) and phobias (e.g. spiders).

Structure of Thought

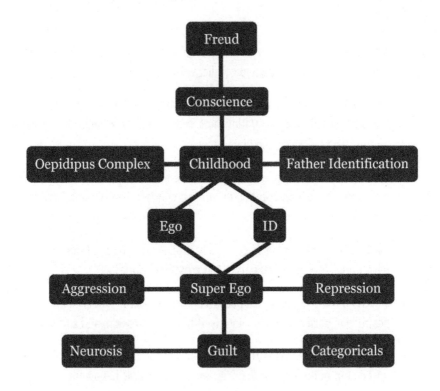

Freudian Revolution

Sigmund Freud (1856-1939) is the **FATHER OF PSYCHOANALYSIS** through his theories of how the conscious and unconscious mind develop and interact. He believed in the **ENLIGHTENMENT** assumption that science could understand all aspects of human behaviour by observing **A POSTERIORI** how patients respond to **PSYCHOANALYSIS** and by positing **THEORIES** (such as **EGO, ID** and **SUPEREGO**) which provide a **STRUCTURE** of thinking.

CONSCIENCE for Freud was a product of experiences in childhood which result in the creation of a **SUPEREGO** – an internal guide which seeks to calm our fears, order our world and resolve conflicts between **EGO** and **ID**. The conscience (superego) is the representative of the voice of our parents who in early childhood produced feelings of pleasure (approval/being loved) and pain (shame/punishment). Various attachments either dissolve (the **OEDIPUS COMPLEX**) or strengthen (gender identification with mother or father), and failure to reconcile a feeling of inner conflict or suppressed desire can lead to depression and **NEUROSIS**.

The structure of Freud's thinking is given on the opposite page, and his theory is sometimes referred to as a **STRUCTURAL THEORY** of the human mind and consciousness. He explains behaviour in terms of the **UNCONSCIOUS** and the sublimation of desire (for example in ideas of God as **FATHER**), or the repression of desire (such as the **LIBIDO** or sexual desire).

Ego

The child develops a sense of **SELF** in relation to the external world. The **EGO** experiences feelings of pleasure and pain and also conscious and unconscious **DESIRES**. The pain of experience propels us towards change but can arise out of **REPRESSION** of urges which become unconscious.

The sense of self begins in childhood with an **IDENTIFICATION** with either **FATHER** or **MOTHER**. The origins of the relationship with the **MOTHER** are explained by the **OEDIPUS COMPLEX** and with the **FATHER** by a process by which the father (**AUTHORITY FIGURE**) becomes part of the infantile stage of the **SUPEREGO**.

CARL JUNG also proposed an **ELECTRA COMPLEX** in 1913 to explain a girl's psychosexual competition with her mother for possession of her father.

The **EGO** thus assumes a regulatory role - it excludes feelings and memories which don't fit our idea of self. For example, this repression resurfaces in **DREAMS** and also **PHOBIAS** – a fear of spiders, for example, which reflect unconscious sources of anxiety. Freud believed the **EGO** was striving to be moral.

The role of **PSYCHOANALYSIS** is to seek to integrate the "coherent ego and the repressed self which is split off from it" (Freud).

Our behaviour (**ACTION**) is a product of both conscious choices and **UNCONSCIOUS** forces 'which exert a driving force without the **EGO** noticing the compulsion" (Freud). These forces result in behaviour which are driven by a complex **PSYCHIC ENERGY** which can leave the human being baffled and confused by their own behaviour – resulting in a feeling of **ANXIETY** or **GUILT**, and **DEPRESSION** (which Freud called 'melancholia').

Id

The **ID** is the seat of feelings, and passions. It is totally non-moral. The origin of the **ID** lies in our **EVOLUTIONARY** background but also in society itself which has conditioned us over generations.

The **ID** develops two broad categories of desire, according to Freud. **EROS** is the life-instinct, which gives us the desires for food, self-preservation, and sex. **THANATOS** is the death-instinct, which drives desires for domination, aggression, violence and self-destruction. These two instincts are at war within the id, and need to be tempered by ego constraints and by **CONSCIENCE**.

Children learn that authorities in the world restrict the extent to which these desires are satisfied. Consequently, humans create the **EGO** which takes account of the realities of the world and society. The ego Freud referred to as the **REALITY PRINCIPLE**, because our awareness of self and of others is crucial to our interaction with the world around us, and is formed at the age of 3 to 5 years.

Within the **ID** there is a battle going on between **EROS** – the life instinct – and **THANATOS** – the death instinct. **EROS** is the 'mischief-maker' (Freud) – the source of uncontrolled passion and also creativity. It is dominated by the **PLEASURE PRINCIPLE**, and yet not all pleasures are felt as acceptable or 'good'. Hence the irrational guilt that can occur over, for example, masturbation and its presence as a **TABOO** in Christianity. Indeed, **EROS** is often at odds with the demands and **CATEGORICAL IMPERATIVES** (Freud's phrase echoing Kant) of the **SUPEREGO**.

The death-instinct (**THANATOS**) is experienced in the desire to kill the **FATHER** and replace him in the mother's affections in the **OEDIPUS COMPLEX**, but is also present in the destructive desires of the **DEPRESSIVE** or self-harming **NEUROTIC**. The death instinct also emerges in **AGGRESSION**, violence and war. In the individual it can have its final expression in **SUICIDE**. But is the positing of a sexual complex just pseudo-science?

Superego

The **SUPEREGO** represents the **INTERNAL** world of **CONSCIENCE**. *"The superego represents the relationship to our parents"* (Freud) and particularly our **FATHER** as authority figure and source of rules and punishments.

To Freud there is a conflict within the human psyche between **EGO** and **ID** and **EROS** and **THANATOS**. A sense of dread emerges in childhood from a fear of castration, a fear of death and a fear of **SEPARATION** from our parents, particularly a fear of loss of the mother's love. The superego can have a destructive power: causing the **EGO** to feel deserted and unloved, abandoned to an anxious and uncertain world and 'fuelling the death-instinct by making the Ego feel abandoned'. This sense of abandonment and powerlessness resurfaces in **DREAMS** (often of failure or of loss of control).

So the **SUPEREGO** can have both a **POSITIVE** and a **NEGATIVE** role – positive in controlling unbridled and anti-social desires and passions, but also **NEGATIVE** in forming an extreme critical voice "brutally chastising and punishing" with guilt, or shame and ultimately a sense of **SELF-HATRED** which cause self-harm and depression.

We can also experience the **SUPEREGO** as **SAVIOUR** and project our guilt and shame onto a sense of **SIN** and a **FATHER-FIGURE** – whom we call **GOD**, who replaces lost love and provides a **SUBLIMINATION** of our sexual desires. Christianity teaches that we deserve death, but that our place is taken by a substitute, Jesus Christ, who removes the **GUILT** and takes on himself the **PUNISHMENT.** (Isaiah 53 "the punishment that makes us whole is upon him"). The **SUPEREGO** in this way grows into a life and power of its own irrespective of the rational thought and reflection of the individual: it is programmed into us by the reactions of other people.

This 'superego', conscience, restricts humans' aggressive powerful desires (**THANATOS** within the **ID**) which would otherwise **DESTROY** us. So guilt "expresses itself in the need for punishment" (Civilisation and its Discontents 1930:315-6). **ERIC FROMM**, quoting Nietzsche, agrees with Freud's analysis of the destructive nature of the **AUTHORITARIAN** conscience.

> *"Freud has convincingly demonstrated the correctness of Nietzsche's thesis that the blockage of freedom turns man's instincts 'backward against man himself'. Enmity, cruelty, the delight in persecution...- the turning of all these instincts against their own possessors: this is the origin of the bad conscience". Eric Fromm, Man For Himself, 1947:113*

Our superego can lead us to **INTERNALISE** shame, and to experience conflicts between the **ID** desires and the shame emanating from the superego responses. The more we suppress our true feelings, the more that which drives us comes from what Freud described as the **SUBCONSCIOUS**, which like an iceberg lies hidden in the recesses of our minds.

Guilt

Freud believed that the more rapidly the **OEDIPUS COMPLEX** succumbed to **REPRESSION** of our desire for our mother, the stronger will be the domination of the **SUPEREGO** over the **EGO** in the form of a severe and dictatorial **CONSCIENCE**.

So "the tension between the demands of conscience and the actual performances of the ego is experienced in a sense of guilt" (Freud). But guilt can itself be **REPRESSED** and so **UNCONSCIOUS**. Unconscious guilt expresses itself in **NEUROSIS** and other forms of **MENTAL ILLNESS**.

SYNOPTIC POINT Freud sees the structure of our Psyche much as Plato describes it in the analogy of the Charioteer (reason) who seeks to harmonise the twin horses of virtue and passion. A man on horseback (the **EGO**) tries to hold in check the superior strength of the horse (**ID**). But unlike the horseman, the **EGO** uses forces borrowed from the **SUPEREGO** – such as shame and guilt. But a result of this is that **EGO**-identity increasingly fails to represent **ID**-desire. The unfulfilled **ID** resurfaces in sick behaviour or **UNCONSCIOUS** forces (**COMPULSIONS**).

Oedipus Complex

Oedipus so loved his mother that he killed his father and assumed his father's role. Infants start with **MOTHER-ATTACHMENT** which is reinforced by the **PLEASURE PRNCIPLE** as the mother satisfies the infants need for sustenance, love and erotic feeling. The hostility to the **FATHER** gradually subsides in healthy children who become more fully identified with the **MOTHER** (girls) or the **FATHER** (boys) as puberty approaches.

However, a failure to identify successfully with one or other parent can lead to transfer of love (Freud saw this as the origin of **HOMOSEXUAL LOVE**). The **EGO** deepens its relationship with the **ID** in rituals which may be associated with shame, such as masturbation, and fantasies that produce guilt. So the **LIBIDO** can be redirected or even suppressed altogether in a sublimation which we call **RELIGION**.

Ultimately, to Freud, Religion is an infantile projection of our desires and longings onto an image which is an **ILLUSION**. In the Christian Thought paper we study more of this theory in Freud's work, The Future of an Illusion.

Evaluating Freud

Weaknesses

REDUCTIONIST George Klein (1973) argues Freud reduces the human mind to an object of enquiry by positing unprovable theories of how conscious and unconscious processes interact. In so doing he reduces human behaviour to a dualism of 'appropriate' and 'inappropriate' behaviour. Like the criticism levelled at geneticist   **RICHARD DAWKINS** we can see this as a form of scientific reductionism.

OVERSEXUALISED Freud argues that the relationship of child and parent has sexual desire through the development of the **OEDIPUS COMPEX** as a key factor. The success or failure of a child's sexual feelings for one or other parent as key to child development is highly contentious. For example, a boy's father is his mother's lover, but he's also the disciplinarian. So, assuming boys do harbour feelings of fear toward their fathers, is this because they fear castration by a romantic rival or because they're afraid of ordinary punishment?

SAMPLING Freud's sample is primarily Austrian upper-class woman, who manifested hysteria. The sample is too small and gender-biased to be truly scientific and the emphasis on sex reveals the cultural repression of that age. Scholars argue Freud fabricates the claim that "almost all of my women patients told me that they had been seduced by their father". John Kihlstrom comments: "While Freud had an enormous impact on 20th century culture, he has been a dead weight on 20th century psychology. The broad themes that Westen writes about were present in psychology before Freud, or arose more recently, independent of his influence. At best, Freud is a figure of only historical interest for psychologists".

Strengths

REVOLUTIONARY Freud was the first person to analyse and theorise about the human unconscious. His argument that dreams are a key to unlocking the secrets of the subconscious mind, his belief that hypnotherapy could change behaviour and his invention of **TALKING THERAPIES** have fundamentally changed our treatment of mental illness.

SECULAR Freud believed religion was a neurosis based on delusions and projections – for example God is a father-substitute onto whom we project our desire for an authority figure, our fear of death and our sense of abandonment. This to Freud was infantile. Westen (1998:35) argues "the notion of unconscious processes is not psychoanalytic voodoo, and it is not the fantasy of muddle-headed clinicians. It is not only clinically indispensable, but it is good science".

HUMANE Freud treated the whole human personality rather than condemning aspects of it as shameful, evil or unacceptable. He thereby challenged the old religious **DUALISMS** of good versus evil, monster versus hero, to give a humane alternative and offering hope of cure and transformation to those whose lives were blighted by mental health problems.

Key Quotes - Freud

"In the Ego and the Id Freud abandons the simple dichotomy between instinct and consciousness and recognizes the unconscious elements of the ego and superego, the importance of nonsexual impulses (aggression or the 'death instinct'), and the alliance between superego and id, superego and aggression". Christopher Lasch *The Culture of Narcissism page 32*

"While Freud had an enormous impact on 20th century culture, he has been a dead weight on 20th century psychology. The broad themes were present in psychology before Freud, or arose in more recently independent of his influence. At best, Freud is a figure of only historical interest for psychologists." John Kihlstrom

"When we were little children we knew these higher natures of our parents, and later we took them into ourselves". Freud

"All that is repressed is unconscious, but not all that is unconscious is repressed". Freud

"To the ego, living means the same as being loved". Freud

"By setting up the superego, the ego has mastered the Oedipus Complex and placed itself in subjection to the Id". Freud

"The tension between the demands of conscience and the performance of the ego is experienced as guilt". Freud

"As the child was once under the domination of its parents, so the ego submits to the Categorical Imperative of the superego". Freud

"Human megalomania will have suffered its third and most wounding blow from the psychological research of the present time which seeks to prove to the ego that it is not even master in its own house". Freud

Evaluation - Psychological Approaches

These psychological accounts of conscience undermine **AQUINAS'** religious theory of conscience (see below) because conscience is **ENVIRONMENTALLY INDUCED** by upbringing, not innate.

Freud's theory is highly **DETERMINISTIC**, because humans are driven, according to Freud, by forces operating out of our subconscious minds.

PSYCHOLOGY doesn't rule out the possibility that God has some involvement with conscience (in originating a moral faculty, for example), but if environment operates so strongly on conscience the religious theories need reworking.

A Theology of Conscience

Key Terms

- **CONSCIENTIA** Aquinas' definition of conscience as 'reason making right decisions".

- **SYNDERESIS** Aquinas' definition of conscience as our innate ability and desire to orientate ourselves towards good ends (aim at the **PRIMARY PRECEPTS**).

- **PHRONESIS** Practical wisdom or right judgement.

- **VINCIBLE IGNORANCE** Blameworthy ignorance of something which we should in principle know about eg a 30 mph zone.

- **INVINCIBLE IGNORANCE** Ignorance which we can't be blamed for - eg a Borneo tribesman's ignorance of Jesus Christ.

St **PAUL** argued that all human beings, Jew and Gentile (non-Jew), possessed an **INNATE** knowledge of God's law, (we're born with it) written on our hearts. *"I do not do the thing I want, the very thing I hate is what I do"* he wrote in **ROMANS 7** and Gentiles have God's law *"engraved on their hearts"*, (Romans 2:15).

John Henry **NEWMAN** (1801-1890) was an Anglican priest who converted to Rome. How could a good Catholic accept papal **INFALLIBILITY** and still follow his conscience? Newman describes conscience as the innate **VOICE OF GOD** and **ABORIGINAL** (= original or native) **VICAR OF CHRIST**.

"It is a principle planted in us before we have had any training" argued Newman. *Newman quoted the fourth Lateran Council when he said "he who acts against conscience loses his soul".* John Henry Newman

AQUINAS (1224-1274) agrees with St Paul and with Newman, as he distinguished between an innate source of good and evil, **SYNDERESIS** (literally, one who watches over us) and a judgement derived from our reason, **CONSCIENTIA**. This second idea is, however, closer to **JOSEPH BUTLER**.

Synderesis and Conscience

Thomas Aquinas saw **SYNDERESIS** (first of two words for conscience) as an innate instinct for distinguishing right from wrong that orientates **DESIRE** and forms the **WILL**. Synderesis can be defined as:

"A natural disposition of the human mind by which we instinctively understand the first principles of morality". Aquinas

Aquinas (optimistically) thought people tended towards goodness and away from evil (the **SYNDERESIS** principle). This principle is the starting point or **FIRST PRINCIPLE** of Aquinas' **NATURAL LAW** system of ethics. So these 'first principles' are the **PRIMARY PRECEPTS** which we observe rational human beings pursue as goals. These include preservation of life, ordered society, worship of God, education and reproduction (acronym **POWER**).

Structure of Thought

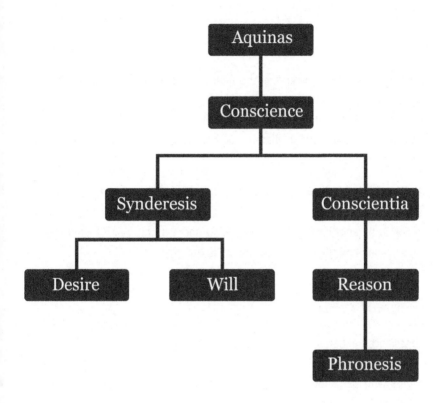

CONSCIENTIA is the power of reason for working out what is good and what is evil, the *"application of knowledge to activity"* (Aquinas). This is something closer to moral judgement rather than instinct, close to Aristotle's **PHRONESIS** or practical wisdom or **BUTLER**'s determining processs for distinguishing between **SELF-INTEREST** and **BENEVOLENCE**. We cannot flourish without it. In practical situations we have to make choices and to weigh alternatives, and we do so by using our conscience. One way we do this is by looking at consequences and applying the **PRINCIPLE OF DOUBLE EFFECT** (when we have to kill a foetus to save a mother's life we have a good intention but a double effect of one good and one evil consequence).

Conscience can make mistakes and needs to be trained in wisdom. At times people do bad things because they make a mistake in discriminating good from evil. Aquinas believed that if the conscience has made a **FACTUAL** mistake, for example, if I don't realise that my action breaks a particular rule, then my mistaken conscience is not to blame.

But if I am simply **IGNORANT** of the rule (such as not committing adultery), I am to blame. Taking a rather bizarre example, Aquinas argues that if a man sleeps with another man's wife thinking she was his wife, then he is not morally blameworthy because he acted "in good faith".

"Conscience is reason making right decisions and not a voice giving us commands". Aquinas

Conscience deliberates between good and bad. Aquinas notes two dimensions of moral decision making, "Man's reasoning is a kind of movement which begins with the understanding of certain things that are naturally known as **IMMUTABLE** principles without investigation. It ends in the intellectual activity by which we make judgements on the basis of those principles". Aquinas

So **SYNDERESIS** is right **INSTINCT** or habit, the natural tendency humans have to do good and avoid evil. **CONSCIENTIA** is right **REASON**, which distinguishes between right and wrong as we make practical moral decisions. We see how conscientia works itself out in the **PRINCIPLE OF DOUBLE**

EFFECT, when we solve a genuine moral dilemma, when two 'good things' conflict and we can't have both.

Vincible and Invincible Ignorance

INVINCIBLE IGNORANCE occurs when people (such as non-Christians or tribes in Borneo) are ignorant of the moral law not because they refuse to believe, but rather because they've not yet had an opportunity to hear and experience it. St. Thomas Aquinas discusses the topic in his Summa Theologica 1-1 Q97. Pope Pius IX used the term in his 1854 document Singulari Quadam .

In his 1963 sermon, "Strength to Love," Martin Luther King wrote, *"Nothing in all the world is more dangerous than sincere ignorance and conscientious stupidity."* Intentional **VINCIBLE** ignorance is when I deliberately act on ignorance. For example, if I choose to fire my rifle into a forest without first making sure there's no-one in the undergrowth picking blackberries, I am "vincibly" ignorant and morally culpable for my actions if I wound someone.

Joseph Butler - Innate Conscience Guided by Reason

Butler (1692-1752), former Bishop of Durham, believed human beings had two natural rational guides to behaviour: enlightened self-interest and conscience. Greeks like **EPICURUS** would have recognised the self-interest of the pursuit of **HAPPINESS**, but not the idea of an **INNATE** (inborn) disposition of conscience.

Butler believed we were naturally moral, and that conscience was the **SUPREME AUTHORITY** in moral actions. Morality was part of our human natures.

Human nature has a **HIERARCHY OF VALUES** with conscience at the top which than adjudicates between the self-love and **BENEVOLENCE** (= doing good to others) which define us as human beings. Conscience helps the selfish human become virtuous and so provides a **BALANCE** between these two tendencies.

Butler doesn't deny we have feelings and passions, but it is conscience which **JUDGES** between them as the "moral approving and disapproving faculty" and we act **PROPORTIONATELY** (appropriately to the situation) according to our conscience.

The guidance is **INTUITIVE**, given by God but still the voice of **REASON**. He is arguing that each human being has direct insight into the **UNIVERSAL** or objective rightness or wrongness of an action.

Evaluation - Butler

Butler attacked the **EGOISM** of Thomas Hobbes. **BENEVOLENCE** is as much part of our shared human nature as **SELF-LOVE**. Here there are echoes of Richard **DAWKINS'** argument that we all share a biologically evolved "altruistic gene" (altruism = concern for others).

Butler sees an **OBJECTIVE MORAL ORDER** in the world. Fortune and misfortune are not entirely arbitrary – if we choose **VICE** we naturally suffer misfortune. Following the dictates of conscience usually leads to **HAPPINESS**. But in the end it's **GOD** who guarantees the consequences turn out best.

"Although Butler's description of conscience is **UNSURPASSED**, he gives no definition of conscience". D.D.Raphael

> "Common behaviour all over the world is formed on a supposition of a moral faculty; whether called conscience, moral reason, moral sense, or divine reason; whether considered as a sentiment of understanding, or as a perception of the heart". Joseph Butler

Authoritarian Conscience - Eric Fromm

Eric **FROMM** experienced all the evil of Nazism and wrote his books to reflect on how conscience and freedom can be subverted even in the most civilised societies. In order to explain how, for example, Adolf **EICHMANN** can plead at his trial for mass murder in 1961 that he was only "following orders" in applying the final solution, we can invoke Fromm's idea of the authoritarian conscience.

The authoritarian conscience is the **INTERNALISED VOICE** of the external authority, something close to Freud's concept of the superego considered above. It's backed up by fear of punishment, or spurred on by admiration or can even be created because I idolise an authority figure, as Unity **MITFORD** did Adolf Hitler.

As Unity found, this blinds us to the faults of the idolised figure, and causes us to become **SUBJECT** to that person's will, so that "the laws and sanctions of the externalised authority become part of oneself" (1947:108).

So, as with the Nazis, ordinary seemingly civilised human beings do **ATROCIOUS EVIL** because they are subject to a voice which comes essentially from outside them, bypassing their own moral sense. This authoritarian conscience can come from:

PROJECTION onto someone of an image of perfection.

The experience of parental **RULES** or expectations.

An adopted **BELIEF** system, such as a religion, with its own authority structure.

> *"Good conscience is consciousness of pleasing authority, guilty conscience is consciousness of displeasing it".* Eric Fromm (1947:109)

The individual's **IDENTITY** and sense of security has become wrapped up in the authority figure, and the voice inside is really someone else's voice. This also means **OBEDIENCE** becomes the cardinal virtue, and as the Nazi Adolf Eichmann pleaded at his trial. **AUTONOMY** and **CREATIVITY** are lost.

> *"Those subject to him are means to his end and, consequently his property, and used by him for his purposes."* Fromm (1947:112)

DESTRUCTIVE TENDENCIES emerge, Fromm stresses, where "a person takes on the role of authority by treating himself with the same cruelty and strictness" and "destructive energies are discharged by taking on the role of the authority and dominating oneself as servant". (1947:113)

> *"Paradoxically, authoritarian guilty conscience is a result of feelings of strength, independence, productiveness and pride, while the authoritarian good conscience springs from feelings of obedience, dependence, powerlessness and sinfulness".* Fromm (1947:112)

The Humanistic Conscience

The **HUMANISTIC** conscience, Fromm suggests is "our own voice, present in every human being, and independent of external sanctions and rewards" (1947:118). Fromm sees this voice as our **TRUE SELVES**, found by listening to ourselves and heeding our deepest needs, desires and goals.

> "Different from the authoritarian conscience is the "humanistic conscience"; this is the voice present in every human being and independent from external sanctions and rewards. Humanistic conscience is based on the fact that as human beings we have an intuitive knowledge of what is human and inhuman, what is conducive of life and what is destructive of life. This conscience serves our functioning as human beings. It is the voice which calls us back to ourselves, to our humanity". Eric Fromm

The result of so listening is to release **HUMAN POTENTIAL** and creativity, and to become what we potentially are; "the goal is productiveness, and therefore, happiness" (1947:120). This is something gained over a life of learning, reflection and setting and realising goals for ourselves.

Fromm sees **KAFKA**'s "The Trial" as a parable of how the two consciences in practice live together. A man is arrested, he knows not on what charge or pretext. He seems powerless to prevent a terrible fate - his own death - at the hands of this alien authority. But just before he dies he gains a glimpse of another person (Fromm's more developed **HUMANISTIC CONSCIENCE**) looking at him from an upstairs room.

Key Confusions

1. "Conscience is a form of consciousness". No, conscience is only a form of consciousness if it is clearly an exercise of choice and reason, as in Aquinas' **CONSCIENTIA** or Butler's principle of judgement between self-interest and benevolence. But Freud argues **UNCONSCIOUS** forces drive guilt feelings which drive conscience - and these forces may be irrational or **NEUROTIC**.

2. "Without God there can be no human conscience". Only in a certain (narrow) Christian world view that sees even our moral sense corrupted by sin. To Aquinas we all share in **SYNDERESIS** which means conscience is a **UNIVERSAL** phenomenon we possess by virtue of our creation in the **IMAGE OF GOD**. It doesn't matter if we believe in God or not.

3. "Science cannot explain conscience". Richard **DAWKINS** would disagree. The **SELFISH GENE** is actually the **SELF-PRESERVING** gene and evolution has given us a genetic predisposition to **ALTRUISM**. So when the conscience of a distinguished Leeds surgeon caused him to jump into the surf off Cornwall to try to save two teenaged swimmers in distress in 2015, he was showing the **ALTRUISTIC** (help others) gene. He tragically died in this heroic moral action.

Possible Future Exam Questions

1. Critically evaluate the theories of conscience of Aquinas and Freud.

2. "Conscience is given by God, not formed by childhood experience". Critically evaluate this view with reference to Freud and Aquinas.

3. "Conscience is a product of culture, environment, genetic predisposition and education". Discuss

4. "Conscience is another word for irrational feelings of guilt". Discuss

5. "Freud's theory of conscience has no scientific basis. It is merely hypothesis". Discuss

6. 'Guilt feelings are induced by social relationships as a method of control". Discuss

Key Quotes - Conscience

"Freud has convincingly demonstrated the correctness of Nietzsche's thesis that the blockage of freedom turns man's instincts 'backward against man himself'. Enmity, cruelty, the delight in persecution - the turning of all these instincts against their own possessors: this is the origin of the bad conscience". Eric Fromm

"Conscience does not only offer itself to show us the way we should walk in, but it likewise carries its own authority with it, that it is our natural guide, the guide assigned us by the Author of our nature; it therefore belongs to our condition of being, it is our duty to walk in its path". Joseph Butler

"Conscience is reason making right decisions and not a voice giving us commands". Aquinas

"The Gentiles can demonstrate the effects of the law engraved on their hearts, to which their own conscience bears witness". Rom 2.15

"Conscience is the built in monitor of moral action or choice values". John Macquarrie

Suggested Reading

Aquinas Summa Theologica 1-1 Q79 (see peped.org/conscience/extracts)

Freud, S. The Ego and the Id Createspace Independent Publishing Platform (22 Mar. 2010)

Fromm, E. (1947) Man for Himself: An Inquiry into the Psychology of Ethics London: Routledge, IV.2

Internet Encyclopaedia of Philosophy, Sigmund Freud, http://www.iep.utm.edu/freud/ (See peped.org/conscience/extracts)

Kihlstrom, John F. (2015). Personality (Pearson) and The Psychological Unconscious. In L.R. Pervin & O. John (Eds.), Handbook of personality, 2nd ed. (pp. 424-442). New York: Guilford. http://socrates.berkeley.edu/~kihlstrm/PersonalityWeb/Ch8CritiquePsychoanalysis.htm

Macmillan, M.B. (1996).Freud evaluated: The completed arc. Cambridge, Ma.: MIT Press.

Strohm, P. (2011) Conscience: A Very Short Introduction, Oxford University Press, Chapters 1 and 3

Westen, D. (1998). The Scientific Legacy of Sigmund Freud. Psychological Bulletin,124, 333-371

Sexual Ethics

Issues Surrounding Sexual Ethics

What does it mean to be **HUMAN**? Is there one **UNIVERSAL** shared human nature (as **NATURAL LAW** suggests)?

Are gender equality and same sex attraction equally ethical issues? Or do we evaluate them as good or bad in the light of **CONSEQUENCES** and **HAPPINESS** produced by social policy and individual action, as the **UTILITARIANS** suggest?

What values give meaning to sexual relationships (such as fidelity, chastity and commitment – which seem to be changing)? Are the **VIRTUES** of human character a better way of analysing this issue?

How have developments in understanding the biology and **PSYCHOLOGY** of the human person affected sexual ethics? Sexual ethics thus shares concerns and insights from **PSYCHOLOGY, BIOLOGY**, and **SOCIOLOGY**. With the prevalence of pornography, sex trafficking and decline in old models of family life, there can be few more pressing ethical issues facing us. The specification identifies three issues:

- **PRE-MARITAL SEX**

- **EXTRA-MARITAL SEX (ADULTERY)**

- **HOMOSEXUALITY**

Structure of Thought

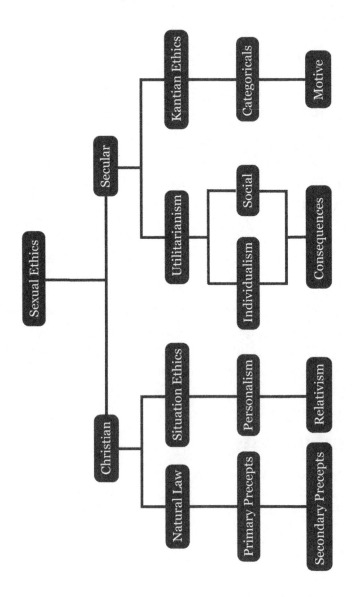

Sex & Evolution

Homo Sapiens emerged around 150,000 years ago. As social life developed so a primitive **MORALITY** created rules and boundaries around sexual intercourse. Sex changes its function from **REPRODUCTION** to **SOCIAL REGULATION**.

Religions emerge that created **PURITY CODES**. These involved **TABOOS** (the declaration of certain practices as unclean). For example the purity code of the Hebrew Bible, **LEVITICUS**, lays down a code of uncleanness – which included **BLOOD, INCEST, ADULTERY**, and **SAME SEX RELATIONS**. These are abominations punishable by social exclusion or death.

Such attitudes are reflected in attitudes to **WOMEN**. Women came to be seen as **PROPERTY** of men. Virginity was prized. Up to 1872, married women in Britain had to surrender all property to their husbands; there was no concept of marital rape until 1991 and violence against married women was only outlawed in 1861. In 2011 there were 443 reported incidents of "honour crime" (violence, forced marriage and even murder) in the UK.

A concept of what is **NATURAL** emerged and with it psychological **GUILT** for those who did not conform. It's hard to believe that in 1899 **OSCAR WILDE** was jailed for two years hard labour for a homosexual relationship. **HOMOSEXUAL SEX** was only legalised in 1967. The last people to be executed for sodomy in England were James Pratt (1805–1835) and John Smith (1795–1835), in November 1835.

Kinsey & the Sexual Revolution

The **KINSEY REPORT** of 1945 shocked America. Intimate surveys of real people's preferences revealed:

- 10% of men were homosexual for at least three years of their lives. How then could sexual preference be **UNCHANGING**, fixed and uniform?

- 26% of married women had extramarital experiences of different sorts.

- 90% of men masturbated.

- 50% of men had been unfaithful to their wives.

Christian Views on Sex

NATURAL LAW

Aquinas taught that there were three rational ends of sex, arising from the **PRIMARY PRECEPT** of reproduction:

- To have children.

- To give **PLEASURE**.

- To bind husband and wife together.

His view – that sex was for pleasure, was widely condemned, Aquinas wrote "the exceeding pleasure experienced in sex does not destroy the balance of nature as long as it is in harmony with reason". Right reason involves a delicate balance of the three purposes of sex – and avoidance of irrational or animal extremes. So the following sexual sins were forbidden:

- **RAPE**

- **CASUAL SEX**

- **ADULTERY**

- **HOMOSEXUAL SEX**

- **MASTURBATION**

Aquinas' view echoed the erotic celebration of sexual ecstasy in the **SONG OF SONGS** in the Hebrew Bible where sex is a sacred gift and picture of a mystical union, and one of the highest spiritual as well as physical forms of being.

Behold you are beautiful, my love;

behold you are beautiful;

your eyes are like doves,

Behold you are beautiful my beloved, truly lovely....

Your two breasts are like two fawns,

twins of a gazelle that feed among the lilies...

You have ravished my heart with a glance of your eyes .

(Song of Songs 1:15; 4:2, 5 & 9)

This is one of two parallel strains in the Bible – one positive and one negative, and the positive strain, that sex is to be **CELEBRATED** is echoed by Jesus himself, quoting Genesis 2:24, "from the beginning God created them male and female, and for this reason a man shall leave his mother and father and be united with his wife, and the two shall become one flesh. So what God has joined together, let no-one divide" (Mark 10:6-9). See also Paul in Ephesians 5:31.

THE NEGATIVE STRAIN - THEOLOGY OF THE FALL

There is also a negative strain in Christianity which sees sex as dangerous, unclean, and sexual pleasure as sinful.

AUGUSTINE wrote that marriage was the *"first fellowship of humankind in this mortal life"*, and *"good not just for producing children, but also because of the natural friendship between the sexes"*, although primarily *"a remedy for weakness, and source of comfort"*. Ultimately the good of marriage lay in its *"goodness, fidelity and unbreakable bond"*.

Augustine argued against the **PELAGIANS** who saw sexual pleasure as a **NATURAL GOOD**, evil only in excess. Augustine agreed with Paul that since the **FALL** the body had been subject to death, *"our body weighs heavy on our soul"* with its sinful desires. Augustine believed that since the fall desire had been tainted by **LUST**. So sexual pleasure in marriage needed to be moderated by reason.

Sexual desire ("the carnal appetite") outside marriage, and sexual activity that results, *"is not good , but an evil that comes from original sin"*. This evil of carnal lust can invade even marriage – so it is **DANGEROUS** and needs to be treated wisely and carefully.

After the **FALL** (Genesis 3) men and women were *"naked and ashamed"*. The man's member is *"no longer obedient to a quiet and normal will"*. Humankind was in danger of running away with lust for each other.

CONCLUSION: Augustine argues that precisely because the body is created good, it can be used wrongly, and this goodness has been deeply stained by the Fall. Sexual desire has to be circumscribed by **MODESTY**, chastity and wisdom.

CATHOLIC TEACHING TODAY

The Roman Catholic Church teaches that sex has two functions – procreative and **UNITIVE** (binding two people together). Procreation is primary. According to Humanae Vitae (1967) these two elements are **INSEPARABLE**.

> *"Sexuality becomes fully human when it is integrated into the relationship of one person to the other in lifelong gift of a man to a woman"*. Catechism 2338

CHASTITY is the virtue of self-mastery (Catechism 2339). It is expressed in friendship towards our neighbour. Sex outside marriage is *"gravely contrary to the dignity of persons and of human sexuality which is naturally ordered to the procreation of children"*. Catechism 2354

HOMOSEXUAL ACTS are "intrinsically disordered". *"They are contrary to the natural law. They close the sexual act to the gift of life. Under no circumstances can they be approved"*. Catechism 2358

ADULTERY is absolutely forbidden by the sixth commandment and Jesus' words.

CONTRACEPTION - in 1951 Pope Pius XII officially permitted the rhythm method, but otherwise **HUMANAE VITAE** (1967) upholds the view that anything that breaks the natural relationship between sex and conception is wrong.

Evaluation - Catholic View

Professor Peter **GOMES** of Harvard University argues that the Bible bans one **CULTURAL** expression of homosexuality – a   promiscuous one and *"never contemplated a form of homosexuality in which loving and faithful persons sought to live out the implications of the gospel with as much fidelity as any heterosexual believer"*. *The Good Book (1997)*

The Catholic interpretation of **NATURAL LAW** implies that the primary function of sex is reproduction. But suppose the primary purpose is **BONDING**, then the argument that sex is purely for reproduction falls down – we can be Natural Law theorists and disagree about the secondary precepts (which Aquinas always argues are relative).

The Catholic **ASSUMPTION** (following Aquinas) is of one human nature. But psychology suggests there are varieties of human nature (heterosexual, homosexual, bisexual) because of genes or environment.

The prohibition on **CONTRACEPTION** seems irrational in a world of overpopulation and **STD**s. If **PRESERVATION OF LIFE** conflicts with **REPRODUCTION**, surely preservation of life is the primary **PRIMARY PRECEPT**?

Situation Ethics - Christian Relativism

Joseph **FLETCHER** sees his own theory as **RELATIVISTIC** (even though it retains one absolute principle, agape love) because any decision is made relative to circumstances.

ABSOLUTE rules must be rejected as authoritarian and unloving.

Biblical prescriptions should be followed as wise **ADVICE** but abandoned in extreme situations if love demands it.

Fletcher argues that many applications of morality are never discussed in the Bible: "Jesus said nothing about birth control, homosexuality, pre-marital intercourse , homosexuality, sex play, petting or courtship". (Fletcher, page 80).

> "It seems impossible to see any sound reason for any of the attempts to legislate morality. It is doubtful whether love's cause is helped by any of the sex laws that try to dictate sexual practices for consenting adults". (Fletcher, Situation Ethics, page 80)

AGAPE love (unconditional love) is the only norm. The situationist is not a 'what asker', ("what sexual practice is allowed?) but a 'who asker'. It's about **PERSONALISM** – people come first.

Evaluation - Situation Ethics (Christian Relativism)

AGAPE is too high a standard for our personal relationships, usually governed by self-interest. Why should I be loving (rather than pleasure-seeking)?

The vulnerable (young, homeless, poor) need the protection of laws preventing **ABUSE** and **EXPLOITATION**.

We cannot predict **CONSEQUENCES** eg unwanted pregnancies or **STD**s happen to people not expecting them who may honestly believe they love the other person.

Homosexual Acts - a Test Case

We have already seen that the Catholic Church condemns homosexual behaviour as intrinsically disordered because of the assumption of one **UNIFORM HUMAN NATURE**. The situationist takes the opposite view; such legalism is unloving and so wrong. Is there a middle way?

In the **ANGLICAN** church there are two gay bishops (in America) and many practising gay priests. **VIRTUE ETHICS** indicates there is a third way of analysing homosexual behaviour. Which **VIRTUES** are present in the relationship? The **EXCESS** of promiscuity is condemned, but faithfulness, care and compassion can apply in any relationship irrespective of orientation. By the same argument the **DEFICIENCY** of abstinence is also a character **VICE**.

The moral issue surrounding homosexuality should therefore be about the promiscuous lifestyle and irresponsible spread of disease (as with heterosexuals). The legalism of natural law or over-emphasis on the code of Leviticus blinds us to the true moral question. What **VALUES** do we need in order to **FLOURISH**?

Kant on Sex

Kant asks us to commit to build the moral world – the **SUMMUM BONUM** or greatest good, by following the rational principle he calls the **CATEGORICAL IMPERATIVE**. This principle has to be applied in all similar circumstances without conditions – it is **ABSOLUTE**. We have to act in such a way that we can imagine a universal law where everyone follows the rule that is generated.

Humans have intrinsic **VALUE** as "ends in themselves". We must be given equal dignity and respect as autonomous rational beings.

We share an irrational nature of passions and instincts with **ANIMALS** but we can rise above these and order our lives by reason. Human sex will be different from animal urges.

LUST disturbs reason. By desiring someone simply as an object of pleasure (rather than seeing them as a whole person, with dignity and reason) we dishonour them and violate their special uniqueness as a free person. We sink to the level of animals.

> *"Sex exposes mankind to the danger of equality with the beasts...by virtue of the nature of sexual desire a person who sexually desires another person objectifies that person..and makes of the loved person an object of appetite. As soon as that appetite is satisfied one casts aside the person as one casts aside a lemon that has been sucked dry".*
> Kant, Lectures on Ethics

MARRIAGE is the best expression of our sexuality. The pleasure of sex is acceptable (ie not animal) because two people surrender their dignity to each other and permit each other's bodies to be used for this purpose — it is a mutual **CONSENSUAL CONTRACT**. Reproduction is not the end of sex, Kant argues, but lifelong surrender to each other in a context of love and respect.

Evaluation of Kant

Kant appears to separate our **ANIMAL** nature from our **RATIONAL**. This dualism explains why he still sees sex as something belonging to the animal nature. But **FEELINGS** and **REASON** cannot be separated this way, many would argue.

Kantian ethics produces **ABSOLUTES** (Categoricals). So the absolute "no sex before marriage" applies here. But in the modern era such absolutes seem to deny the possibility of a **TEMPORARY** committed relationship – or even sex for fun.

It's possible to be a Kantian and accept **HOMOSEXUAL MARRIAGE** but not **ADULTERY**.

Utilitarianism - Balancing the Positive and the Negative

What do the utilitarians say about our four issues: contraception, pre-marital sex, adultery and homosexuality? Here we contrast two utilitarians: **MILL** (1806-73) and **SINGER** (1946-).

Mill is a **MULTILEVEL** utilitarian who follows a more **ARISTOTELEAN** idea of happiness – **EUDAIMONIA** or personal and social flourishing. He argues that we need **RULES** to protect justice and **RIGHTS**, which are the cumulative wisdom of society. But when happiness demands it, or a **CONFLICT** of values occurs, we revert to being an **ACT** utilitarian – hence multilevel (Act and Rule) utilitarianism.

Mill agreed that **CONTRACEPTION** was moral as it increased personal and social happiness, through family planning and restrictions on population growth. Today the British Humanist association writes "if contraception results in every child being a wanted child and in better, healthier lives for women, it must be a good thing". Mill was imprisoned in 1832 for distributing "diabolical handbills" advocating contraception.

Mill had found a murdered baby in a park. The practice of exposing unwanted children was widespread. Hospitals for **FOUNDLINGS** such as **CORAM** set up in Bristol in 1741, did little except institutionalise **INFANTICIDE** (child killing). Between 1728 and 1757 33% of babies born in foundling hospitals and workhouses died or were killed.

On **HOMOSEXUAL** rights Mill follows Bentham in arguing for "utilitarian equality" by which everyone's happiness counts equally. Bentham was the first philosopher to suggest legalised **SODOMY** in an unpublished paper in 1802. Freedom was a key to personal flourishing, and as long as no harm was done to any but consenting adults, (Mill's **HARM PRINCIPLE** in On Liberty) it is a private matter how people order their sex lives.

In his essay on **LIBERTY** (1859) Mill argues for **SOCIAL RIGHTS** so we can undertake "experiments in living" that give us protection from the prejudices of popular culture and "the tyranny of prevailing opinion and feeling". Mill would have approved of **COHABITATION** and pre-marital sex.

Evaluation - Mill

Mill was a father of the **LIBERALISM** we take for granted where difference is tolerated. His brand of utilitarianism balances social **JUSTICE** and individual freedom and pursuit of happiness.

Utilitarianism works well looking **BACKWARDS**. The Abortion Act (1967), the Homosexual Reform Act (1967) and the Divorce Reform Act (1969) are all examples of utilitarian legislation.

Utilitarian ethics works less well looking forwards. We cannot predict **CONSEQUENCES**. So the **AIDS** epidemic can be seen as a product partly of personal freedom to adopt a promiscuous "unsafe" lifestyle. It is hard to see how a utilitarian can prevent this or even argue it is wrong if freely chosen.

Many of the greatest **SOCIAL** reforms have not been inspired by Christian values, Natural Law or Kantian ethics, but by **UTILITARIAN** considerations of social **WELFARE**. Today relatively few Christian churches accept the complete equality of women.

Preference Utilitarianism

Peter Singer defends the utilitarian line advanced by Mill and argued that, with **HOMOSEXUALITY**, *"If a form of sexual activity brings satisfaction to those who take part in it, and harms no-one, what can be immoral about it?"*

On **ADULTERY** preference utilitarians approve of any sexual activity which maximises the preferences of individuals, taking account the preferences of all those affected. So incest, bestiality, or adultery would all be acceptable.

Singer as argues for **CONTRACEPTION** as population growth is one of the most pressing utilitarian issues, we should "help governments make contraception and sterilisation as widespread as possible" (Practical Ethics, page 183). But overseas aid should be made conditional on adoption of contraceptives.

Key Confusions

- "Sexual ethics is merely up to individual choice". It is a common misunderstanding of ethics that it is purely about personal choice. Yet **MILL** points out, following **ARISTOTLE**, that ethics always has a personal and a social dimension. Laws both reflect social morality and also help to mould it. So when the law was changed on homosexuality, contraception and child protection it both reflected a change in social attitudes (things once thought acceptable are now seen to be abusive and other things once criminalised are now morally accepted) and helped to form those attitudes. And if I choose to be promiscuous that affects every person I am promiscuous with.

- "Sexual behaviour is natural and doesn't do anyone any harm". This is a misunderstanding of what 'natural' means in ethics. For example, the word 'natural" in **NATURAL LAW** means 'in line with our rational natural purpose'. Certain goals are unique to human beings - for example **WORSHIP OF GOD** and even those shared with animals (**REPRODUCTION**) function in a different way to animals - we are **MORAL** beings capable of evaluating consequences, for example, and capable of understanding our social responsibility to build an orderly and co-operative society.

- "There is one heterosexual human nature". This is an **ASSUMPTION** of natural law theory which appears highly questionable. It seems there really is a **HOMOSEXUAL** human nature and also a **TRANSGENDER** human nature. The whole ethics of sexual behaviour has altered radically in the light of empirical research (such as the **KINSEY** report) and also the insights of psychologists such as **FREUD** and **JUNG**. Moreover the criticisms of a type of religious thought that equates sex with **SIN** may well still hang over in the **GUILT** that attends certain expressions of sexual behaviour. Of course, which expression is part of our ongoing ethical debate.

Possible Future Exam Questions

1. "Religion is irrelevant in deciding issues surrounding sexual behaviour". Discuss

2. Critically evaluate the view that the ethics of sexual behaviour should be entirely private and personal.

3. "Because sexual conduct affects others, it should be subject to legislation". Discuss

4. "Normative theories are useful in what they might say about sexual ethics". Discuss

Key Quotes - Sexual Ethics

"The only purpose for which power can be rightfully exercised over any member of a civilised community against his will, is to prevent harm to others. His own good, either physical or moral, is not sufficient warrant". JS Mill

"If a form of sexual activity brings satisfaction to those who take part in it, and harms no-one, what can be immoral about it?" Peter Singer

"The pleasure derived from the union between the sexes is a pleasure: therefore, leaving aside the evils, which derive from that source here is why the legislator must do whatever is in his power so that the quantity in society is as high as possible". Jeremy Bentham

"Sex exposes mankind to the danger of equality with the beasts...by virtue of the nature of sexual desire a person who sexually desires another person objectifies that person..and makes of the loved person an object of appetite. As soon as that appetite is satisfied one casts aside the person as one casts aside a lemon that has been sucked dry ". Kant

"It seems impossible to see any sound reason for any of the attempts to legislate morality. It is doubtful whether love's cause is helped by any of the sex laws that try to dictate sexual practices for consenting adults". Joseph Fletcher

Suggested Reading

Aquinas On Marriage Summa Theologica II-II   Q153 a. 2c, a. 3c, q. 154 a. Extract available on Peped's sexualethicsteachingresources.co.uk website)

Pope Paul VI (1968) Humanae Vitae (Available on Peped's sexualethicsteachingresources.co.uk website)

Church of England House of Bishops (1991) Issues in Human Sexuality, London: Church House Publishing

Mill, J.S. (1859) On Liberty, Chapter 1

Religious Pluralism and Theology

Background

Christianity has always existed alongside other religions. In its growth out of **JUDAISM**, Christians had to decide the extent to which they would continue with beliefs and practices of others, and what was it that was going to make them distinctively Christian. The question of whether other religions contain valuable truths remains, as well as the extent to which Christians can be seen to have a unique **EXCLUSIVE** relationship with God. Issues within religious pluralism and society also arise, for example, should Christians work to convert others or is it possible for non-Christians to achieve salvation too.

Specification

At A level, you will need to explain and evaluate the teaching of contemporary Christian theology of religion on exclusivism, inclusivism, and pluralism. You need to show knowledge and understanding of:

1. The view that only Christianity fully offers the means of salvation

2. The view that although Christianity is the normative means of salvation, 'anonymous' Christians may also receive salvation

3. The view that there are many ways to salvation, of which Christianity is one path (OCR A Level in Religious Studies Specification, 2016, p. 36)

Key Terms

- **EXCLUSIVISM:** the view that only one religion offers the full means of salvation

- **INTER-FAITH DIALOGUE:** discussing religious beliefs between members of different religious traditions, with an intention of reaching better understanding

- **THEOLOGY OF RELIGION:** a branch of Christian theology that considers the relationship between Christianity and other world religions from a Christian perspective

- **INCLUSIVISM:** the view that although one's own religion sets the standard (is 'normative') for means of salvation, those who accept its fundamental principles may also attain salvation

- **PLURALISM:** the view that there are several means of salvation through different religious traditions

- **PARTICULARISM:** another name for exclusivism, meaning that salvation can only be found in one particular way

- **VATICAN II:** the Second Vatican Ecumenical Council, held from 1962 to 1965 to deliberate the place of the Catholic Church in the modern world

- **NOUMENA:** a Kantian term to describe reality as it really is, unaffected by the human mind

- **PHENOMENA:** a Kantian term to describe reality as it seems to us, filtered by the human mind

Structure of Thought - Religious Pluralism

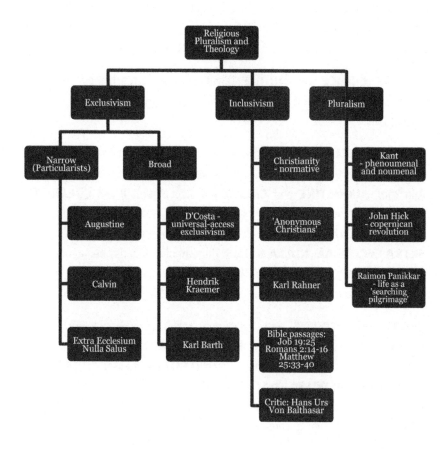

Christian Teaching on Exclusivism

EXCLUSIVISM is the belief that only Christianity offers the means of salvation. It comes from the belief that Jesus is 'the' way, not 'a' way to salvation. Another word for exclusivism is **PARTICULARIST**.

Christ's **SACRIFICE** was **UNIQUE**. Salvation can only reach those who hear the gospel and respond to this with faith. A sign of this acceptance is **BAPTISM**.

NARROW EXCLUSIVISM is the belief that salvation is possible only for those of a particular Christian denomination (Baptist, Catholic, Lutheran, Anglican). **AUGUSTINE** and **CALVIN** are examples of **PARTICULARISTS**. They believed God only elects – through grace - a small number of Christians for salvation. **Catholics** believe there is no salvation outside of the Church – **EXTRA ECCLESIAM NULLA SALUS**. The Catholic view has been considered less narrow since **LUMEN GENTIUM** – "many elements of sanctification and of truth are found outside of its visible structure" (1964).

BROAD EXCLUSIVISM is the belief that salvation is possible for all who accept Christ, regardless of denomination. Other religions may contain some truth, but not enough for salvation. Gavin **D'COSTA** asserted **UNIVERSAL-ACCESS EXCLUSIVISM** – that salvation is possible after death. **1 TIMOTHY 2:3-4** supports this – "this is good, and pleases God our Saviour, who wants all people to be saved and to come to a knowledge of the truth".

HENDRIK KRAEMER – The Christian Message in a Non-Christian World. Kraemer was part of the **ECUMENICAL MOVEMENT** aiming to bring different Christian denominations together. Worked among missionaries in non-Christian countries, spreading the message that salvation could only be achieved by converting to Christianity. We should evaluate religions

HOLISTICALLY to see if 'as a whole', the religion accepts Christ's salvation or not.

KARL BARTH – Church Dogmatics. Emphasised the importance of Christ for salvation. Humans cannot achieve salvation on their own. Presents **'THEOLOGY OF THE WORD'** – God can only be known where He chooses to reveal this knowledge through His Word – through Christ's life, death, and resurrection; through the Bible and through Church teaching. Revelation is always God's choice. **CHRIST** is the **FULLY UNIQUE** way God has chosen to reveal himself and so is the only fully reliable way of gaining knowledge of God.

Christian Teaching on Inclusivism

INCLUSIVISM is a middle path between exclusivism and pluralism. Christianity is a **NORMATIVE** means of salvation but **'ANONYMOUS'** Christians may also receive salvation (Karl **RAHNER**).

Salvation can be reached by people who turn to Christ in the **AFTERLIFE**. Salvation is possible for those who follow God sincerely, albeit in a wrong religious context. Truth in other religions could be from Christ – even if they do not recognise this.

KARL RAHNER – Christianity sets the **STANDARD** by which other religions should be measured. An **OMNIBENEVOLENT** God should be able to offer salvation to those who have not been able to freely accept Christ. Christianity holds the truth, but people can follow Christ unknowingly. People who do not know Christ can still have a relationship with God – e.g. **JOB 19:25**. Such people are called **ANONYMOUS CHRISTIANS**.

HENDRIK KRAEMER - disagreed with Rahner. **NON-CHRISTIAN RELIGIONS** were **CULTURAL CONSTRUCTS**, not responses to God's revelation through Christ.

The **BIBLE** can be seen as a source of authority:

1. **JOB 19:25** – Job appears to refer to Jesus – "I know that my redeemer lives".

2. **ROMANS 2:14-16** – non-believers can have an innate sense for Christ, even if they do not recognise it – "They show that the requirements of the law are written on their hearts".

3. **MATTHEW 25:33-40** – the Parable of the Sheep and the Goats implies anyone living by altruistic love is working for Christ – whether they realise it or not. "What you do for the least person, you do for me" says Jesus.

HANS URS VON BALTHASAR – CRITIC of the '**ANONYMOUS CHRISTIAN**'. Multi-culturalism should not be an excuse to 'water down' the importance of Christ's crucifixion and resurrection.

Christian Teaching on Pluralism

PLURALISM is the view that there are many ways to salvation. Christianity is one of these. Human culture causes differences in beliefs and practices, but religions share the same ultimate goal.

KANT – there is a difference between the **NOUMENAL WORLD** (world as it really is) and the **PHENOMENAL WORLD** (world as it appears to us). Nature of God belongs to the noumenal world.

JOHN HICK – called for a **'COPERNICAN REVOLUTION'** in theology: to put God central – not Christianity. This call **AWAY FROM** a **CHRISTOCENTRIC** approach to theology is driven by our observations of the world, just as the **COSMOLOGICAL COPERNICAN REVOLUTION** was.

Religion is a **PHENOMENAL** attempt to understand God (by experience). All religions fall short of the truth. Christianity's 'truth claims' e.g. Virgin Birth, should be understood as myths expressing human relationship with 'the **REAL'**. God is **BENEVOLENT** and so salvation must be extended to all.

Hick's call for **DEMYTHOLOGIZATION** of the Bible has origins in **RUDOLF BULTMANN**. This is the idea that the Gospels do contain essential truths but these are revealed through **MYTHS**.

Hick argues it is impossible to create rational arguments for God e.g. **NATURAL THEOLOGY**. People are given reason to believe by **RELIGIOUS EXPERIENCES**. Knowledge of God is similar to our other knowledge of the world – through our experiences. Since individual experiences provide the grounding for belief, we must respect all religions, since none of them can provide universally-accepted argument for their beliefs. Experiences of God can be interpreted through the lens of different religions and faith is how we interpret these events. An **ANALOGY** is how different people respond differently to the same **MUSICAL STIMULUS**, influenced by their cultural background. Cultural influences might explain the differences in how people interpret the divine. Human projection shapes the experience but does not cause it.

Challenges to Pluralism

Supporting Hick

- **FEUERBACH -** religious belief is projection. No genuine external cause of the religious experience

- **CUPITT -** challenges existence of God

- **PHILOSOPHICAL ARGUMENTS** – if 'the Real' is unknowable, we can't say anything meaningful about it and it cannot reveal itself deliberately to humans – this would make the revelation come from the human mind.

- Hick's theology allows for a **GLOBAL** theology and does not exclude polytheistic or non-theistic religions

Opposing Hick

- **INCARNATION** is regarded as central to Christianity, affirmed in the creed. Hick challenges traditional doctrines.

- **CHRISTIANS** might argue Hick undermines the essence of Christianity and reduces the Bible to fiction with morals.

- **LEE STROBEL** – 'the Case for Christ' – the gospels are eyewitness documents. But we know very little of Jesus' early life and the gospels were written after Jesus' death.

CONCLUSION OF HICK's PLURALISTIC HYPOTHESIS Empirical evidence, practical considerations and philosophical logic lend themselves to a Copernican revolution in theology.

How Was Hick Influenced by Kant?

The distinction between **NOUMENA** and **PHENOMENA** helps us to comprehend how different religions are talking about the same reality (noumena) but do so in different ways since our mind shapes our perception of our experiences (phenomena).

SYNOPTIC connection **PLATO** (Forms) -> **KANT** (noumena) -> **HICK**

RAIMON PANIKKAR – we need to be 'open' about the truth, rather than making claims about it. Life is a **'SEARCHING PILGRIMAGE'** and we might need to let go of traditions in order to find our identity. **CHRISTOPHANY** is God's way of making Himself known to people. **RELIGIOUS PLURALISM** is a **SPIRITUAL POSITION** not an intellectual position.

Confusions to Avoid

1. Hick is NOT calling for one religion with everyone having the same beliefs – **GLOBAL THEOLOGY** is NOT the same as a **GLOBAL RELIGION**. He is emphasising that people necessarily have different ways of experiencing the divine.

2. Hick is NOT saying all religions are correct – rather, that they **CONTAIN TRUTH**. They also contain human projection and error and since we cannot know all truth, we must respect all religions.

3. For the belief system to be valid, it ought to lead people away from selfishness and towards ethical living. Therefore, not every belief system reflects the Divine.

Possible Exam Questions

1. "A theologically pluralist approach significantly undermines the central doctrines of Christianity." Discuss.

2. To what extent can non-Christians who live morally good lives and genuinely seek God be considered to be 'anonymous Christians'?

3. Critically assess the view that only Christianity offers the means of salvation

4. "Christianity is one of many ways to salvation." Discuss.

Key Quotes

"Those also can attain to salvation who through no fault of their own do not know the Gospel of Christ or His Church, yet sincerely seek God and moved by grace strive by their deeds to do His will as it is known to them through the dictates of conscience". (Catechism, paragraph 19)

"I know that my redeemer lives, and that in the end he will stand on the earth" Job 19:25

"All that matters (metaphysically) is that Jesus did rise from the dead, and that this act made salvation possible for all, irrespective of one's particular religion." (Religion, Key Concepts in Philosophy, 2007, p. 154)

"This is good, and pleases God our Saviour, who wants all people to be saved and to come to a knowledge of the truth". (1 Timothy 2:3-4)

"They show that the requirements of the law are written on their hearts". *(Romans 2:14-16)*

"Whoever believes in him is not condemned, but whoever does not believe stands condemned already because they have not believed in the name of God's one and only Son." *(John 3:18)*

"For it is by grace you have been saved, through faith—and this is not from yourselves, it is the gift of God— 9 not by works, so that no one can boast." *(Ephesians 2:8-9)*

"You see that a person is considered righteous by what they do and not by faith alone." *(James 2:24)*

Suggested Reading

Hick's official website:
http://www.johnhick.org.uk/jsite/index.php/articles-by-john-hick

Philosopher Kings website:
http://www.philosopherkings.co.uk/hickandpluralism.html

Hick, J. (1995) God and the Universe of Faiths, SCM Press, Chapters 1 and 10

McGrath, A. (2010 5th Edition) A Christian Theology, Wiley-Blackwell, Chapter 17

D'Costa, G. (2009) Christianity and World Religions, Wiley-Blackwell

Religious Pluralism and Society

Background

In the 21st Century, a question that concerns many Christians is how they relate to people who follow no religion, or non-Christian beliefs. This goes together with the **MULTI-CULTURALISM** of Britain, leading it to become a multi-faith society. Issues arise for a Christian who might ask themselves whether to tolerate, or try to convert other people. Issues of religious expression in the workplace and attitudes towards sexuality have also made the public eye in the media. Christians might be unsure of how to voice their opinion without being discriminatory. Some Christians have become involved in **INTER-FAITH DIALOGUE**.

Specification

At A level, you will need to explain and evaluate:

1. The development of contemporary **MULTI-FAITH** societies – the reasons for this development, for example, migration

2. Christian responses to, including:

   a. Responses of Christian communities to inter-faith dialogue

   b. The scriptural reasoning movement (its methods and aims; and how the mutual study and interpretation of different religions' sacred literature can help understanding of different and conflicting religious truth claims)

3. How Christian communities have responded to the challenge of encounters with other faiths, for example:

   a. Catholic Church: **REDEMPTORIS MISSIO (ENCYCLICAL**, pp. 55-57)

   b. Church of England: Sharing the Gospel of Salvation (OCR A Level in Religious Studies Specification, 2016, p. 37)

Key Terms

- **ENCYCLICAL** an open letter sent by the Catholic hierarchy to the churches, endorsed by the Pope

- **MISSIONARY WORK** activity that aims to convert people to a particular faith or set of beliefs, or works for social justice in areas of poverty or deprivation

- **MULTI-FAITH SOCIETIES** societies in which there are significant populations of people with different religious beliefs

- **SOCIAL COHESION** when a group is united by bonds that help them to live together peacefully

- **SYNOD** the legislative body of the Church of England

Structure of Thought - Pluralism and Society

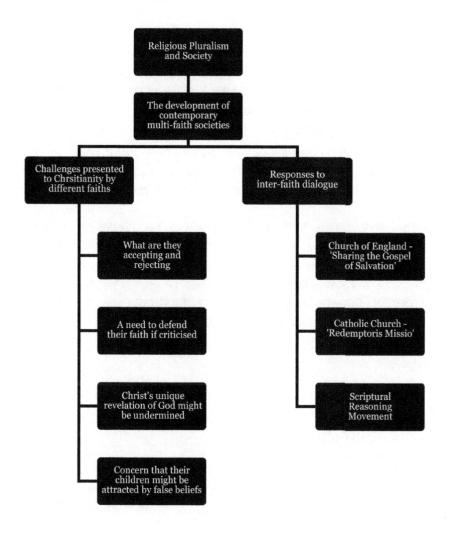

The Development of Multi-Faith Societies

Example - Migration

Christianity was introduced by the **ROMANS**. Before this, religious practices concentrated around worship of ancestors, fertility and agriculture. Christianity was established as the **PRIMARY FAITH** in Britain in **7th CENTURY**. Western development in **TRAVEL** and **COMMUNICATION** has increased **CULTURAL** and **RELIGIOUS DIVERSITY**. In the 1950s and 60s, the Textile industry was short of labour - encouraging immigration from **PAKISTAN** and the **CARIBBEAN**. **IDI AMIN** expelled the **ASIAN** population from **UGANDA** in 1972. This led to arrival in Britain of **HINDUS, MUSLIMS** and **SIKHS**.

People have travelled more for holiday and work and this has led to greater contact with different beliefs and traditions. 'Pockets' of religious groups were caused by religious people choosing to live near where others who practised the same religion. **SIKHS** arriving in 1950s for work tended to settle in **LONDON, BIRMINGHAM** and **WEST YORKSHIRE**; while the **JEWISH** population is higher in **NORTH LONDON** and **LEEDS**. When travelling, local etiquette needs respecting and for this, further education about beliefs is also needed.

MAX MULLER'S 19th century translations of Hindu texts into English (**THE SACRED BOOKS OF THE EAST**) increased interest in meditation and ideas such as **REINCARNATION**.

The changes have resulted in **MIXED-FAITH MARRIAGES,** the teaching of world faiths in schools, people working among **RELIGIOUS DIVERSITY**, the stocking of multi-faith **FESTIVAL FOODS** in supermarkets, **PRAYER ROOMS** in airports and hospitals, and an acceptance of **ATHEISM** and

AGNOSTICISM, allowing religious beliefs to also be challenged.

Some argue that this new opportunity for the sharing of beliefs has helped to dispel prejudice and to **PROMOTE PEACE**. Others say it has helped **DEEPER REFLECTION** on one's own beliefs; while others still, claim tolerance is promoted at the expense of the **UNIQUE MESSAGE** of **SALVATION** through **CHRIST** promoted by the Christian mission.

Responses to Inter-faith Dialogue

Inter-faith dialogue is also known as inter-belief dialogue and inter-religious dialogue. It aims for mutual peace, respect, and cooperation. It aims to understand:

- Common ground and points of difference

- One's own faith while learning about, and from, beliefs of others

It is NOT about **CONVERSION** but serves renewed interest in the wake of migration and human responses to tragedies such 9/11.

David Ford: The Future of Christian Theology

Inter-faith dialogue has new direction due to two major historical strands:

1. **HOLOCAUST**: the role played by Christianity in spurring on anti-Semitism in contrast with those that opposed Nazism. **DABRU EMET** (**'SPEAK THE TRUTH'**) – was an invitation from Jewish leaders to Christians, calling for **CO-OPERATION**.

2. Rising **TENSIONS** between Islam and the West: **A COMMON WORD BETWEEN US AND YOU** – a call from Muslim leaders to Christianity outlining the responsibility of both to work for the common good of all.

Catholic Church - Redemptoris Missio (Mission of the Redeemer)

JOHN PAUL II – encouraged perseverance with the Christian mission in a multi-faith world. **PAPAL ENCYCLICALS** – letters from the Pope to Church leaders, are considered to be an authority and a 'final word.' **REDEMPTORIS MISSIO** (1990) re-visited the issues of **VATICAN II** and affirmed the essential place of Christian mission in a multi-faith world.

All religions provide spiritual opportunity, despite gaps and errors. The **LAITY** understand Christianity as lived through everyday life and so have a key role in dialogue.

All **CATHOLICS** have a duty to engage in **RESPECTFUL DIALOGUE**. This dialogue gives an opportunity to bear witness and is an 'expression' of Christian mission – not an opposition to it. The unique path to salvation through Christ is still offered by Christianity and should be emphasised.

Church of England - Sharing the Gospel of Salvation

1. **'THE DIALOGUE OF DAILY LIFE'** – informal discussions of differing beliefs

2. **'THE DIALOGUE OF THE COMMON GOOD'** – different faiths cooperate to help the community

3. **'THE DIALOGUE OF MUTUAL UNDERSTANDING'** – formal debates e.g. Scriptural Reasoning

4. **'THE DIALOGUE OF SPIRITUAL LIFE'** – meet for prayer and worship

This **FOURFOLD PLAN** to **SHARING THE GOSPEL OF SALVATION** is in response to **PAUL EDDY'S** 2006 question asking the Church to clarify the position of the Church of England on converting others. The plan affirmed that Jesus uniquely offers salvation and the Church of England has a mission to testify to this.

Christians should make efforts to speak about their beliefs openly and honestly but should not treat this as a 'marketing' exercise. Conversions are God's work – not the result of a 'good sell'.

Christians should make efforts to engage with members of different faiths – **MORE THAN JUST TOLERANCE.** Christians should follow the **GOLDEN RULE** – to 'treat others as you would like to be treated' (**LEVITICUS 19:18**) and should listen to others and leave judgement to God.

The Scriptural Reasoning Movement

How the mutual study and interpretation of different religions' sacred literature can help understanding of different and conflicting religious truth claims.

The movement began as a **JEWISH ACADEMIC FORUM** in the USA. In the mid-1990s, Christians asked to join to learn and found the conversations to be engaging. **MUSLIMS** were asked to join because of shared roots (**COMMON**

GROUND) and together, the three religions can be known as **RELIGIONS OF THE BOOK** because each religion claims to have a holy text that is authoritative and revelatory. The movement now welcomes people of **ALL FAITHS**.

Cambridge Inter-faith Forum

This involves a discussion of themes considering scriptures of the Abrahamic faiths (those that come from a common origin in the **HEBREW** Scriptures) – Judaism, Christianity, Islam. Discussions are held in English in order to be inclusive. Discussions will concern earning, clothing, modesty, fasting, differing truth claims (e.g. Prophethood and Trinity) among other topics. The forum will consider how beliefs that appear similar are understood in their own contexts. Honesty and openness are encouraged.

Strengths

Brings together people of different faiths, aiding **TOLERANCE** in a multi-faith society.

IDEAS - Collaboration socially and academically is encouraged.

Face-to-face discussion is encouraged, as well as joint research. This further promotes inter-religious harmony and **SOCIAL COHESION** through raised awareness and understanding of one's own views and those of others.

Weaknesses

INDIVIDUALISTIC - Participants represent themselves – it is possible we lose sight of the normative teaching of each religion.

It is difficult to decide if an interpretation is **REASONABLE**.

It is **QUESTIONABLE** – the extent to which theological **EXCLUSIVISTS** can engage fully in inter-faith dialogue.

Although open to all faiths, the extent to which non-Abrahamic faiths with varied origins and traditions can partake fully and benefit, is questionable.

Some will criticise the **RELATIVIZING** of religious groups by treating all beliefs as equally valid.

Confusions to Avoid

1. There is some debate as to whether conversion of those of no faith is significantly different to conversion of those of a previous faith. On the one hand, those converting from a previous faith might face bigger challenges because of their **FAMILY** and social group.

2. This tension might not be the same for someone of no religious background – thought, their social group might change. On the other hand, some **INCLUSIVISTS** might argue that the non-religious have a greater need to know God than the 'anonymous Christian' does. The non-religious might never have encountered the opportunity to become religious; while others might have actively opposed religion.

Possible Exam Questions

1. To what extent should Christians seek to convert others to Christianity at every opportunity?

2. "Inter-faith dialogue is of little practical use." Discuss.

3. To what extent does scriptural reasoning relativise religious beliefs?

4. "Converting people of no faith should be equally important to a Christian as converting people of non-Christian faith." Discuss.

Key Quotations

From Redemptoris Missio (paragraphs) and the Bible:

"Every person has the right to hear the 'Good News' of the God who reveals and gives himself in Christ" Para. 46

"In the light of the economy of salvation, the Church sees no conflict between proclaiming Christ and engaging in inter-faith dialogue" Para. 55

"The Church gladly acknowledges whatever is true and holy in the religious traditions of Buddhism, Hinduism and Islam as a reflection of that truth which enlightens all people" Para. 55

"Dialogue should be conducted and implemented with the conviction that the Church is the ordinary means of salvation and that she alone possesses the fullness of the means of salvation" Para. 55

"Dialogue leads to inner purification and conversion" Para. 56

"Inter-religious dialogue is a part of the church's evangelising mission" Para. 55

"Therefore go and make disciples of all nations, baptising them in the names of the Father and of the Son and of the Holy Spirit." (Matthew 28:19)

Suggested Reading

The Doctrine Commission of the Church of England (1995) The Mystery of Salvation Church House Publishing, Chapter 7

Ford, D. (2011) The Future of Christian Theology, Wiley-Blackwell, Chapter 7

Pope Paul VI (1965) Nostra Aetate; Declaration on the relation of the Church to non-Christian religions

The Challenge of Secularism

Background

The role of religion in Western Europe has changed and is changing. Christianity in Britain has been in decline – seen in Church attendance and solemnisation of fewer marriages. This reduction has led to questions from **PSYCHOLOGY** and **SOCIOLOGY** about the role of religious institutions in public life and culture. It has been suggested that religion should be seen as part of the **'PRIVATE'** rather than 'public' sphere while the relationship between Christianity and British culture is diminishing.

Specification

At A level, you will need to explain the rise of **SECULARISM** and **SECULARISATION**, and know and evaluate:

1. The views that God is an illusion and the result of wish fulfilment

2. The views of Freud and Dawkins that society would be happier without Christianity as it is infantile, repressive and causes conflict

3. The views that Christianity should play no part in public life

4. The views of **SECULAR HUMANISTS** that Christian belief is personal and should play no part in public life, including education and schools, and government and state (OCR A Level in Religious Studies Specification, 2016, p. 40). Be aware that there are two different approaches to secularism, and one of these argues that **SECULARISM**

is absolutely necessary for religious toleration and diversity, (the other, argued by **DAWKINS**, argues that religion should be completely excluded form public life).

Key Terms

- **SECULAR** not connected or associated with religious or spiritual matters

- **SECULARISM** various meanings – a belief that religion should have no role in public or government life; a belief that no one religion should have a superior position in the state; a belief in a public space and a private space, and that religion should be kept apart from public power

- **SECULARISATION** a theory rising out of Enlightenment thinking, developed in the 1950s and 1960s, that proposed that with the advancement of democracy and technology, religious belief would progressively decline. Such a linear decline is now doubted by sociologists

- **WISH FULFILMENT** according to Freud, the satisfaction of a desire through a dream or other exercise of the imagination

Structure of Thought - Challenge of Secularism

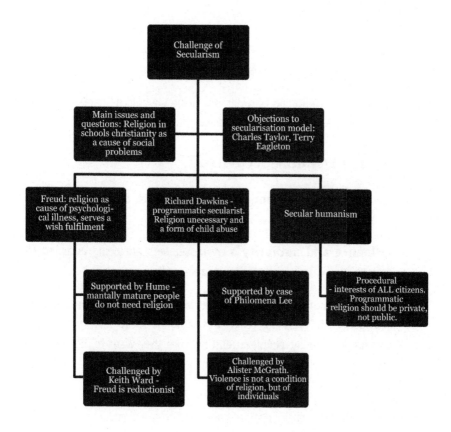

Challenge of Secularism

Main issues and questions: Religion in schools christianity as a cause of social problems

Objections to secularisation model: Charles Taylor, Terry Eagleton

Freud: religion as cause of psychological illness, serves a wish fulfilment

Richard Dawkins - programmatic secularist. Religion unecessary and a form of child abuse

Secular humanism

Supported by Hume - mantally mature people do not need religion

Supported by case of Philomena Lee

Procedural - interests of ALL citizens. Programmatic - religion should be private, not public.

Challenged by Keith Ward - Freud is reductionist

Challenged by Alister McGrath. Violence is not a condition of religion, but of individuals

The Rise of Secularism and Secularisation

Important Aims to Understand

1. Reasons for the rise of secularism and secularisation and the views that God is an illusion and the result of wish fulfilment

2. The views of Freud and Dawkins that society would be happier without Christianity as it is infantile, repressive and causes conflict

Difficulty in Defining Secularism

1. **Measuring and defining terms**: less Church attendance does not mean less spirituality

2. **Influence and authority**: new movements are being accepted by society, even with a decline in mainstream religions

3. **Religious commitment and evidence of the past**: Church attendance in previous years was not the best test of religious commitment. Today, people attend because they want to, not because they must. So, what really is an appropriate way of measuring secularisation?

AUGUSTE COMPTE - civilised society develops progressively from:

1. *Theological* perspective

2. *Metaphysical* (abstract) view of the world

3. *Positive* (scientific/rational) view of the world

Sigmund Freud

Religion is a key cause of **PSYCHOLOGICAL** illness. Tradition and conformity **REPRESS** natural instincts, and this leads to **NEUROSES**.

Freud considered that religion belongs to the **INFANTILE** – belief is formed in the early stage of human social development. This stage is before the person has developed the ability to reason and at this stage, needs external care and security provided by a **FATHER** and **MOTHER** figure (by **PROJECTION**, God and the Virgin Mary).

Supported by Hume

Mentally mature people do not need religion – it is practised by the uneducated.

Freud went further to say that religion was a **SICKNESS** and could be proven as such by his use of psychoanalysis.

When instinctual life wins and religion ends, humans will be content.

Wish Fulfilment

As children, there is a **VULNERABILITY** and helplessness that is fulfilled 'by a belief that injustices will be corrected, that life has a purpose, and that there is a moral code' (Freud, The Future of an Illusion). God – or belief in God – represents a **PERSONIFICATION** of our needs. Religion can answer questions that humans have that cannot be answered by studying 'what is real?'

Religion causes conflict as it creates unreliable and harmful answers to human uncertainty and matters outside of our control.

Challenges to Freud

KEITH WARD labels Freud a **REDUCTIONIST** because he appears to reduce everything to material terms. This is an **INADEQUATE** explanation for the spiritual experience of existence.

Truth claims about religion cannot be disproved.

Freud emphasises the **DESTRUCTIVE** nature of religion but for others, religion is an aide rather than a harm. It can assist understanding and acceptance of life. Religion can help to form communities rather than to divide them.

Freud **GENERALISES** religions – while some are hierarchical and controlling, not all are and therefore, not all religions can be seen to perpetuate guilt.

Wish fulfilment might not always lead to illusion – it can lead to creativity such as that seen in **DREAMS** and daydreams.

Richard Dawkins - Programmatic Secularism

In **THE GOD DELUSION**, Dawkins makes the case for:

1. Imagining a world without religion

2. Accepting that the God hypothesis is weak

3. Realising that religion is a form of child abuse

4. Accepting atheism with pride

Dawkins argued that life can be meaningful without reference to religion. The processes of nature can be most clearly explained by Charles Darwin and his

THEORY of **EVOLUTION**.

Belief in God is **DELUDED** and unnecessary. Religion is delusional since it represents a persistent false belief going against the main body of evidence. The supernatural world cannot be subject to empirical study and therefore, Dawkins rejects **STEPHEN JAY GOULD'S** attempts to argue that religion and science are '**NON-OVERLAPPING MAGISTERIA'**. For Dawkins, all things must be able to be studied empirically. (Link with **VERIFICATIONISM** in Religious Language).

RELIGION IS A FORM OF CHILD ABUSE – A child lacking understanding should not be labelled as religious. Dawkins criticised the state for allowing a child below the age of consent and reason to be labelled as religious. They have been unable to think about the beliefs they are labelled as possessing. This could be seen in school admissions, for example.

Dawkins used the example of **CATHOLICISM** as a form of long-term psychological abuse. He gave the example of Catholic women who had experienced sexual abuse, who found the fear of hell to be greater than the abuse itself. Another example was the '**HELL HOUSE'** thought of by a pastor in Colorado. Here, children were terrified by actors role-playing the sins of abortion and homosexuality, followed by the torture of Hell. Dawkins suggests that the power of belief in religion becomes greater than the physical abuse suffered.

Example- Philomena Lee

Had her child, born out of wedlock, taken from her by the Catholic Church. She stayed with her boy for three years at the **SEAN ROSS ABBEY** in Roscrea – a place for unwed mothers. Philomena's boy was then sold, to be adopted by a Catholic family.

Responses to Dawkins - Alister McGrath

The Dawkins Delusion

Many Christians think faith is not irrational. Furthermore, religion and science are not necessarily in conflict. Science can explain the intelligible universe and so **DAWKINS** is right to criticise the '**GOD OF THE GAPS'**. However, the intelligible universe could still point to an intelligent designer.

The relationship between science and religion can be **COMPLEMENTARY**, reflecting different aspects of human experience.

Dawkins' **LIMITED POSITIVIST VIEW** that metaphysical questions are outside of scientific enquiry and therefore meaningless is criticised by many scientists. Science, theology and philosophy can provide useful insights.

MCGRATH also criticised Dawkins' claim that violence was a necessary condition of religion. Jesus taught against violence – "turn the other cheek". Violence is a condition of certain individuals, not religion as a whole. McGrath also notes that atheism has also been a part of violence and repression, e.g. in communist regimes.

Secular Humanism - Christian Belief is Personal

Two Types of Secularism

1. **PROCEDURAL**: the interests of ALL citizens – religious and non-religious, should be considered by the state. Religion should be treated equally to other institutions but not with preference.

2. **PROGRAMMATIC**: in a **PLURAL** society, the state should be solely secular. This means religious views and practices should be kept apart from public institutions – schools, universities, public holiday and government.

The main aims of modern humanism were set out in the **AMSTERDAM DECLARATION** of 1952:

1. Humanism is **ETHICAL**: all humans are of worth, have dignity and autonomy

2. Humanism is **RATIONAL**: science should be used imaginatively and as a basis for solving human difficulties.

3. Humanism supports democracy and human **RIGHTS**: the best way in which humans can develop their potential.

4. Humanism insists that personal **LIBERTY** must be combined with **SOCIAL RESPONSIBILITY**: no dogmatic beliefs, the autonomous person has a responsibility to society and the natural world

5. Humanism is a response to the widespread demand for an alternative to dogmatic religion: continuous observation will build our reliable understanding of the world and revision of **SCIENTIFIC** understanding.

6. Humanism values artistic **CREATIVITY** and imagination: enhancing human existence. Novelist **E.M. FORSTER** defined the humanist as someone with "curiosity, a free mind, belief in good taste, and belief in the human race."

7. Humanism is a **LIFESTANCE** aiming at the maximum possible fulfilment: creative and ethical living can help us to achieve the challenges of the present

Education and Schools

Government and State

1776 – Formation of the USA – Church and State made separate.

Keeping Church and State separate might be seen as one way of avoiding conflicting political aims between Christian denominations and even with other religions with the increase in migrants.

Alternative ideas about theocracy are seen in:

1. **DOMINIONISTS**: America should be ruled according to Biblical laws – based on Genesis 1:28 where humans are said to have dominion – this includes over the state. A view held mostly by Protestant, evangelical and conservative groups.

2. **RECONSTRUCTIONISTS**: Similar Dominionist notion. Seen in the Old Testament when the life of Israel was ordered according to laws given to Moses. Followed by Calvinists.

In England, the Queen is the Head of the Church of England. 26 Bishops sit as **'LORDS SPIRITUAL'** in the **HOUSE OF LORDS**. Regardless of faith, church of England Parish Churches can be used for marriages, funerals and baptisms. This is a way of the state providing a spiritual life for everyone.

NOTE: England is NOT a **THEOCRACY.**

Some **PROGRAMMATIC SECULARISTS** believe the government should go further in separating Church and State.

ROWAN WILLIAMS – the Church has a role to play in resisting the apparent threat of secularism felt by some religious fundamentalists who are anti-democratic (as they oppose democratic consensus on laws such as legalisation of abortion and homosexuality reform)

CHRISTOPHER DAWSON – secular education systems bring challenges. They deprive people of the ability and right to make sense of their own culture – a culture which, to a large extent, is immersed in religion.

Objections to the Secularisation Model

CHARLES TAYLOR – the **'SUBTRACTION STORIES'** of **DAWKINS** and **FREUD** show how the world can be explained with stories that show neither God, nor any 'greater being' is needed for us to live fulfilled lives.

This is **'SELF-SUFFICING HUMANISM'**. This humanism fails because it emphasises the individual and in so doing, loses the **COMMUNAL** aspect of society (notice though, a counter-argument, that humanists argue for **SOCIAL RESPONSIBILITY**). Rather than a discovery that God does not exist, our exclusion of God from our explanation of the world reflects a **WESTERN PHASE**. In order to live a full life, we need to embrace a sense of the divine and distance ourselves from secularism.

TERRY EAGLETON – a **MARXIST** and **CHRISTIAN** approach. Marxist in the sense that he thought it wrong to exclude religious imagination and its contribution to human existence. Eagleton thought the harm of religion should be weighed up against its positive contributions.

The **SPIRITUAL** aspect of human experience can be captured by religion, but not by secularism. People have been prepared to make ultimate sacrifices for truths about existence but not for **AESTHETIC** reasons e.g. sport/ music.

Secularist privatisation has seemed to make religion and morality irrelevant. 9/11 showed the dangers of a **POSITIVIST** view of the world without religion where dangerous extremists interpret the Western secularists as trying to turn the world anti-religious.

Key Confusions to Avoid

1. The discussion concerning whether spiritual values are just 'human values' can sometimes lead to confusion. To say spiritual values are just 'human', implies that there is '**NO SIGNIFICANT OTHER**' to which they are directed or from which they come.

2. Arguments to support this include the belief that values often labelled as 'Christian' are actually fundamental values of being human and part of flourishing in society. Such values include those of **COMPASSION, FORGIVENESS, JUSTICE, AND PEACE**. Furthermore, those who argue that these spiritual values are no different to 'being human', might add that the aforementioned values do not require a belief in God or an afterlife in order to be endorsed.

3. On the other hand, there are arguments that spiritual values are much more than simply 'human'. For example, some spiritual values such as self-sacrifice and 'love your enemies' do not always benefit the human. Spiritual values are untainted by human, material desires, and express a commitment to something 'other'. Furthermore, it has been suggested that the **UNIVERSAL DECLARATION OF HUMAN RIGHTS** is based on the belief that humans have 'ultimate worth', and so values are **ABSOLUTE**.

4. Lastly, there is an argument that human and spiritual values cannot be

made separate and this was shown in the **INCARNATION**.

Possible Exam Questions

1. "Christianity has a negative impact on society." Discuss.

2. To what extent are Christian values more than just basic human values?

3. "Christianity should play no part in public life." Discuss.

4. Critically assess the claims that God is an illusion and the result of wish fulfilment.

Key Quotes

"Faith is the root of freedom and programmatic secularism cannot deliver anything comparable". Rowan Williams, Faith in the Public Square, 2012, page 32

"9/11 highlights two extremes of anxiety: faithless Western secular atheism and its fear of religion (and hence its reaction as the 'war on terror') and faithful religious fundamentalism and its fear of positivism, capitalism and secularisation". Michael Wilcockson, Religious studies for A Level Year 2, 2017, page 277

"No, our science is no illusion. But an illusion it would be to suppose that what science cannot give us we can get elsewhere". Sigmund Freud, The Future of an Illusion, 2001, page 56

"The presence or absence of a creative super-intelligence is unequivocally a scientific question". Richard Dawkins, The God Delusion, 2006, page 59

"Dawkins' naïve view that atheists would never carry out crimes in the names of atheism simply founders on the cruel rocks of reality". Alister McGrath and Joanna Collicutt McGrath, The Dawkins Delusion?, 2007, page 78

"There is something infantile in the presumption that somebody else (parents in the case of children, God in the case of adults) has a responsibility to give your life meaning and point." Richard Dawkins, The God Delusion, 2006, p. 404

"The religions of mankind must be classed as among the mass delusions". Sigmund Freud, Civilisation and its Discontents, 1930, page 81

"Children, I'll argue, have a human right not to have their minds crippled by exposure to other people's bad ideas". Nicholas Humphrey, 'What Shall We Tell the Children?' Amnesty Lecture, 21 February 1997,

Suggested Reading

British Humanist Society, https://humanism.org.uk/

Dawkins, R. The God Delusion, Chapter 9

Dawson, C. (1956) 'The Challenge of Secularism' in Catholic World, also online: http://www.catholiceducation.org/en/education/catholic-contributions/the-challenge-of-secularism.html

Ford, D. (2011) The Future of Christian Theology, Wiley-Blackwell, Chapters 3 and 6

Freud, S. The Future of an Illusion

Liberation Theology and Marx

Background

Marx introduced the idea that when humans are unable to live fulfilling lives due to being 'dehumanised', this results in a form of **ALIENATION**. Humans are **DEHUMANISED** when they are **EXPLOITED,** and this is a result of being treated as objects and used as a means to an end.

Marx's teachings on alienation and exploitation have been used by **LIBERATION THEOLOGY** to analyse the **'STRUCTURAL'** causes of **SOCIAL SIN** that have led to poverty, violence, and injustice. Such 'structural' causes include capitalism and institutions (schools, churches, and the state).

The analysis of structural sin has led to a call for the **'PREFERENTIAL OPTION FOR THE POOR'** – a thought calling for Christians to act in solidarity with the poor, rooted in the Gospel. The implication of this teaching is to place **ORTHOPRAXIS** (right action) before **ORTHODOXY** (official Church teaching).

Specification

At A Level, we explain and evaluate liberation theology and Marx, including:

1. Marx's teaching on **ALIENATION** and exploitation

2. **LIBERATION THEOLOGY**'s use of Marx to analyse social sin

3. Liberation theology on the **'PREFERENTIAL OPTION** for the poor'

Key Terms

- **ALIENATION:** The process of becoming detached or isolated

- **BASIC CHRISTIAN COMMUNITIES:** Christian groups that gather to try to directly resolve problems in their lives

- **CAPITALISM:** An economic system in which the means of production are privately owned and operated for profit, in contrast with communism where the state controls trade and industry

- **ORTHODOXY:** Right belief

- **ORTHOPRAXIS**: Right action

- **PREFERENTIAL OPTION FOR THE POOR:** Acting in solidarity with the poor and oppressed

- **STRUCTURAL SIN:** Social dimension of sin, beyond individual sin. It is an attitude of society that contributes to oppression

Structure of Thought - Liberation Theology and Marx

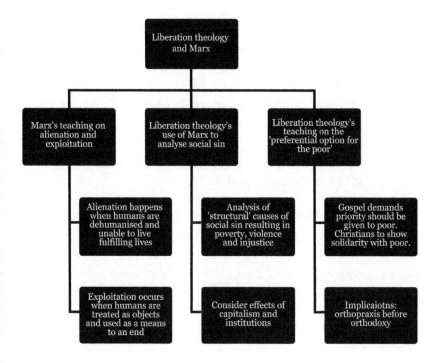

Marx's Teaching on Alienation and Exploitation

Marx taught that alienation occurs when humans are dehumanised and unable to live fulfilling lives. **EXPLOITATION** occurs when humans are treated as objects and used as a means to an end. Note the similarity to Kant's second formulation of the **CATEGORICAL IMPERATIVE** here (treat people not just as a means to an end but always also as an **END** in themselves).

For example, consider a recent purchase from someone you might not know. You might have bought a sandwich from a local supermarket. Did you stop to think about the person serving you at the till? Or, in today's times of 'self-service' – have you thought of the people involved in the building and maintenance of the machines, the famers producing the ingredients needed for the bread and filling of your purchase?

Marx's teaching on **ALIENATION** and exploitation help us to think about the people involved in the **PRODUCTION** of things we value. Marx would say it does matter and should matter that we appreciate the persons involved in the stages of production and do not just see them as a means of production. If we do the latter, we alienate them from society.

Furthermore, technology has revolutionised the world but with the more apparent power we have in this development, the less in control we actually feel. Marx said there is a **HUMAN CAUSE** behind this feeling of powerlessness.

When humans reached the ability to produce **SURPLUS TO REQUIREMENTS**, the favour was granted to those who controlled the means of production and herein begIns class division. This division is evident through the ownership of land, where labour is bought and sold – people are treated as means and not 'ends'. Marx laid the foundations for **SOCIALISM** and

COMMUNISM through his criticism of **CAPITALISM** – the private ownership of land. This private ownership changed the relationship between people and the means of production, leading to the exploitation and alienation of the workers.

What does this look like?

1. **FEUDAL LORDS** own the land and the means of producing food.

2. **SERFS** work on the land but don't own it. They rely on feudal lords for access and must give surplus to feudal lords.

3. **SUBSERVIENT** Serfs alienated from the land on which they work.

This system can be likened to working in a factory. Here, people only understand the part they work on and do not have sight of the whole process. In this way, they are **DEHUMANISED**. The work is necessary as without it, we could not pay for our survival. In this way, exploitation becomes a means to an end. Workers form part of a supply chain and do not know the 'purchasers'.

Neither do those purchasing know the workers - people are **ALIENATED** from their work. Our 'happiness' at cheap prices comes at the expense of other people's happiness - at the expense of the exploitation of others.

Liberation Theology's Use of Marx and Social Sin

Liberation theology began as an **INTELLECTUAL** and **PRACTICAL THEOLOGICAL** movement among those who worked with the poor.

PAULO FREIRE described the process of **'CONSCIENTISATION'** – a process by which someone becomes aware of the power structures in society. **FREIRE**

argued that education should teach people to read the power structures and should work to **TRANSFORM** society and not to just transmit information.

Traditionally, theology had focussed on passing on information. **LIBERATION THEOLOGY** focused on **ACTION** before **EXPLANATION** – **ORTHOPRAXY** before **ORTHODOXY**. Liberation theology became, therefore, a **THEOLOGY OF ACTION**.

Liberation theology proposed that the **KINGDOM OF GOD** is not a place we go to when we die; but is something to work for in this life.

GUSTAVO GUTIÉRREZ, one of the founders of liberation theology, proposed that liberation occurs two-fold:

1. **SOCIAL AND ECONOMIC** – poverty and oppression are the consequence of human choices and therefore humans can resolve as well. Hence an idea of **SOCIAL SIN**.

2. **FROM SIN** – to be reconciled with the Divine.

Both 'social and economic' and 'from sin' aspects of liberation must happen together. Gutiérrez claimed that **POLITICAL LIBERATION** is the work of salvation. He emphasised earthly liberation, whereas **JUAN SEGUNDO** emphasised spiritual liberation.

The Bible extracts in the 'key quotations' section allow you to consider how each teaching might have influenced the development of liberation theology. For example, **MATTHEW 25:40** - "whatever you did for one of the least of these brothers and sisters of mine, you did for me" – encourages the **PREFERENTIAL OPTION FOR THE POOR** in the call to side with **'ONE OF THE LEAST'**, i.e. an outcast.

Liberation theology has its origins in 1960s Latin America, a place of corrupt governments and poverty. Christian groups formed to discuss experiences and practical solutions. Liberation theology therefore became a **THEOLOGY OF HOPE**, with God's love extending both to creation and to liberation.

LATIN AMERICA had found itself at a crossroads, a significant battleground in the cold war conflict between the USA and USSR. Marx had predicted a violent uprising of the oppressed – this seemed to be happening. Liberation theology focused on increasing **HUMAN WELL-BEING** rather than **HUMAN MATERIAL WEALTH**. This links to Marx's understanding that industrialisation can sacrifice the well-being of humans, despite the increase in wealth.

Liberation theology's use of Marx here, seems to be that the process of industrialisation is supported by a structure of sin that then forms part of the organisation of society, and in turn, part of the systems of government and education.

GUTIÉRREZ warned against using every aspect of Marxism but mentions his theories of alienation and exploitation. Gutiérrez also utilises Marx's suggestion that human beings can change the world they inhabit. Gutiérrez considered that people of Latin America wanted to be liberated from capitalism and so he called for the Church to stand with such movements for liberation – **BEING CHRISTIAN NECESSITATES BEING POLITICAL**. Gutiérrez went as far as to say that to not get involved in politics would be equal to helping to keep things the same, even if this situation was wrong/ undesirable.

The **STRUCTURAL SIN** that must be changed can be seen in the injustices experienced by the oppressed. The current social system is one of structural inequality. By failing to address the class struggle, we legitimise the existing system, and in so doing, we act as a part of it. Perhaps Marx's most important contribution to liberation theology is his emphasis on recognising the class struggle against the structures of sin.

Liberation Theology's Teaching on "Preferential Option for the Poor'

The **GOSPEL** demands that Christians must give priority to the poor and act in **SOLIDARITY** with them. Liberation theology demands we put **ORTHOPRAXIS** before **ORTHODOXY**.

The teaching on **PREFERENTIAL OPTION FOR THE POOR** refers to a **BIBLICAL TREND** to show favour to the oppressed and outcasts. This follows the example set by Jesus – "whatever you did for one of the least of these brothers and sisters of mine, you did for me" **(MATTHEW 25:40).** The phrase was first coined by **FATHER ARRUPE, SUPERIOR GENERAL OF THE JESUITS in 1968**, and was later picked up by the Catholic bishops of **LATIN AMERICA. JUAN SEGUNDO** taught that a preferential option for the poor shows an **AUTHENTIC CHRISTIAN RESPONSE**, avoiding the dangers of neutrality.

JUAN SEGUNDO wrote that the Church "intends to struggle, by her own means, for the defence and advancement of the rights of mankind, especially of the poor". Since we are made in **GOD'S LIKENESS, HUMAN DIGNITY** should be central to what we do. By failing to intervene and by allowing an ongoing social divide, we would prove incompatible with the peace and justice advocated in the Bible.

SEGUNDO differed to **GUTIÉRREZ** because he argued that liberation from sin (**SPIRITUAL LIBERATION**) should come before **SOCIAL LIBERATION.**,as social liberation might not be possible. Even Jesus taught *"the poor you will always have with you, but you will not always have me" (Matthew 26:11)*. Segundo still taught we should prioritise the preferential option for the poor - now gained acceptance beyond liberation theology.

JOHN PAUL II used the term in his encyclical **CENTESIMUS ANNUS** (1991). In this, he argued that support of the poor is an opportunity for the moral and cultural growth of humankind. However, this also includes a care for **SPIRITUAL POVERTY** – not just a focus on material wealth:

"This option is not limited to material poverty, since it is well known that there are many other forms of poverty, especially in modern society – not only economic but cultural and spiritual poverty as well". (Centesimus Annus para 43)

This spiritual poverty can be caused by focusing too much on the material goods. **POPE PAUL II** referenced drug and pornography addiction as an indication of a broken social structure. A destructive reading of human needs leaves a spiritual void that is filled by exploitation of the weak. **POPE FRANCIS** encourages the Catholic Church to be a **'POOR CHURCH FOR THE POOR'**.

The **CATHOLIC CHURCH** was concerned about the theological use of Marx as some of Marx's ideas were considered intolerable and thus a danger to use in theology **(CARDINAL RATZINGER).** Furthermore, Ratzinger (later Pope Benedict XVI) also claimed that using Marx interfered with the **EUCHARISTIC CELEBRATION** of power struggle. Evangelism was in danger of being superseded by violent revolution. Christian liberation should focus on **LIBERATION FROM SIN**, with God being the ultimate liberator. Marxism, Ratzinger claimed, was inherently un-Christian.

BONAVENTURE (1221-74), in **TEMPTATIONS FOR THE THEOLOGY OF LIBERATION (1974)**, criticised liberation theology for prioritising action over the Gospel. He claimed that liberation theology equated theology with politics, and as a result, side-lined Christian evangelism. Bonaventure highlighted that liberation theology focused on structural and not personal sin – despite Jesus' emphasis on **PERSONAL RECONCILIATION** with God.

However, for the starving and oppressed, one can question whether liberation from sin is more important than social liberation. Jesus did teach the importance of inner spiritual change, but he also called for real action – seen in the **PARABLE OF THE SHEEP AND THE GOATS (MATTHEW 25)**. The election of a Latin American Pope might signal the beginning of real impact of liberation theology. Pope Francis named **OSCAR ROMERO** a martyr and asked Gutiérrez to be a keynote speaker at a Vatican event in 2015.

However, in a 2017 visit to **MYANMAR** Pope Francis failed to explicitly denounce the persecution of the **ROHINGYA** Muslims by supposedly pacifist Buddhists.

Confusions to Avoid

1. Liberation theology would claim it is not Marxist, but rather, makes use of Marx's analysis of society. Within liberation theology, Marxism is not treated on its own – it is always considered in relation to the situation of the poor. Marxism is of '**INSTRUMENTAL**' use to liberation theology – an instrument in understanding and responding to the needs of the oppressed. For more on this, read **BOFF** in 'recommended reading'.

2. Christianity would claim that its 'preferential option for the poor' came from the Bible and that Marx's criticism of religion was based on corruptions in which the Church had contributed to oppression.

3. Liberation theology's call for **ORTHOPRAXIS** (living) before orthodoxy (dogma) might imply that the church had not advocated Christian action. This is not true. Christianity had always advocated putting beliefs

into practice (see **JAMES** "faith without works is dead'). Liberation theology brought to attention the need of religion to affect the whole life – including an active role in the traditionally more secular areas of politics and **ECONOMICS**. This is what made liberation theology distinctive.

Possible Exam Questions

1. To what extent should Christianity engage with atheist secular ideologies?

2. "Liberation theology has not engaged with Marxism fully enough." Discuss.

3. Critically assess the claim that Christianity has tackled social issues more effectively than Marxism.

4. Critically assess the relationship of liberation theology and Marx with particular reference to liberation theology use of Marx to analyse social sin.

Key Quotes

"The growth of the Kingdom is a process which occurs historically in liberation". (Gutiérrez, A Theology of Liberation, 1973, p. 177)

"Then the Lord said to Moses, "Go to Pharaoh and say to him, 'This is what the Lord, the God of the Hebrews, says: "Let my people go, so that they may worship me." (Exodus 9:1).

He has performed mighty deeds with his arm; he has scattered those who are proud in their inmost thoughts. He has brought down rulers from their thrones but has lifted up the humble. He has filled the hungry with good things but has sent the rich away empty. (Luke 1:51-53)

"Again I tell you, it is easier for a camel to go through the eye of a needle than for someone who is rich to enter the kingdom of God." (Matthew 19:24).

"The King will reply, 'Truly I tell you, whatever you did for one of the least of these brothers and sisters of mine, you did for me.' (Matthew 25:40).

"For my Father's will is that everyone who looks to the Son and believes in him shall have eternal life, and I will raise them up at the last day." (John 6:40).

"Blessed are the poor in spirit, for theirs is the kingdom of heaven. (Matthew 5:3).

Social division whereby the worker "is depressed...both intellectually and physically, to the level of a machine" (Karl Marx, Early Writings, [1833-4] 1975, p.285

"Education is part of the machine of capitalism and pupils are the cogs in that machine" Libby Ahluwalia and Robert Bowie, Oxford A Level Religious Studies for OCR Year 2, 2017, page 305.

"In Latin America to be Church today means to take a clear position

regarding both the present state of social injustice and the revolutionary process which is attempting to abolish that injustice and build a more human order." Gustavo Gutiérrez, A Theology of Liberation, 1974, p. 265;

"It is a will to build a socialist society, more just, more free, and human, and not a society of superficial and false reconciliation and equality." Gustavo Gutiérrez, A Theology of Liberation, 1974, p. 273-412.

"Liberation theology used Marxism purely as an instrument. It does not venerate it as it venerates the gospel". Leonardo Boff and Clodovis Boff, Introducing Liberation Theology, 1987

"Let us recall the fact that atheism and the denial of the human person, his liberty and rights, are at the core of the Marxist theory". Congregation of the Doctrine of the Faith, Instruction on Certain Aspects of the 'Theology of Liberation', 1984, para 7.6

Suggested Reading

Boff, L. and Boff, C. (1987) Introducing Liberation Theology, Burnes and Oates

Gutierrez, G. (1974/2000) A Theology of Liberation, SCM Press, Chapter 4

Congregation of the Doctrine of the Faith (1984) Instruction on certain Aspects of the 'Theology of Liberation'

Wilcockson, M. (2011) Christian Theology, Hodder Education, Chapter 7

Influence of Marx – online resource.
See http://www.philosopherkings.co.uk/Marx.html

Gender and Society

Background

The Christian Church has lagged behind changes in social attitudes (and UK laws) in recent years, particularly on sexual issues such as **CONTRACEPTION, ABORTION** and **PRE-MARITAL SEX,** and gender issues such as attitudes to **HOMOSEXUALITY** (including gay marriage). For example, the Church of England still formally disallows homosexual gay partnerships in the **CLERGY** whilst professing to welcome gay church members. Gender issues also include attitudes to **TRANSEXUALS** and the political implications of **FEMINISM**.

Key Terms

- **ESSENTIALIST THEORIES:** Gender is fixed by objective human nature, either by God or by our inherent biology (eg genes)

- **EXISTENTIALIST THEORIES:** Gender is determined by social discourse (Foucault), by upbringing (Freud), or by social conditioning (including religious conditioning)

- **FEMINISM:** A movement and a philosophy emerging form the Enlightenment emphasis on equal rights, but embracing theories of power and social conditioning.

- **SEX:** Refers to the biological and physiological characteristics that define men and women

- **GENDER:** The state of being classified as male or female or transgender (typically used with reference to social and cultural differences rather than biological ones).

- **FALSE CONSCIOUSNESS:** Beliefs and behaviour induced by social attitudes and values which contradict the true interest (economic, political or social) of a person

- **PATRIARCHY:** A system of society or government in which men hold the power and women are largely excluded from it.

- **ETERNAL FEMININE:** Simone de Beauvoir's term to describe the role of woman as some ideal imposed by men (submissive housewife, sex object etc).

Specification

A Level requires us to study the effects of changing views of **GENDER** and gender roles on Christian thought and practice, including:

- Christian teaching on the roles of men and women in the family and society

- Christian responses to contemporary **SECULAR** views about the roles of men and women in the family and society including reference to:

  - **Ephesians 5:22–33**

  - **Mulieris Dignitatem 18–19**

The ways in which Christians have **ADAPTED** and **CHALLENGED** changing attitudes to family and gender, including issues of:

- motherhood/parenthood

- different types of family (single parent, extended, nuclear etc)

Note: there is not one, but **MANY** Christianities. The specification mentions just one Bible passage of many that need to be taken, and one Roman Catholic Document, Mulieris Dignitatem, in the context of a history of **PAPAL ENCYCLICALS**. Roman Catholics and Evangelical Christians argue against women leadership for different reasons. **QUAKERS** have always espoused strict gender equality and are pacifist.

Gender – Essentialist or Existentialist

ESSENTIALIST gender is essential to biology eg Biblical account of creation "God created them male and female'. Often includes conclusions about roles and/or intelligence eg men are stronger and wiser (**AQUINAS**).

EXISTENTIALIST gender is a product of **CIVILISATION** (de Beauvoir), male expectation, a cultural interpretation of gender roles, or an interpretation of the Bible. E.g. body image is a cultural construction (modern anorexic images very different from Rubens portraits).

Exploitation and Power (Michael Foucault)

The idea that human beings have a **SEXUALITY** is a recent western social phenomenon.

At the start of the 18th century, there was an emergence of "a political, economic, and technical incitement to talk about sex,"with experts speaking about the morality and rationality of sex, fuelled by Catholic teaching on sex, sin and confession" (Foucault).

ENLIGHTENMENT emphasises the empirical nature of sex and gender eg biological differences between men and women, the nature and source of sexual pleasure and supposed **OBJECTIVE** measures of intelligence and emotion

The "world of perversion" that includes the sexuality of children, the mentally ill, and homosexuality all subject to more vigorous prosecution. The labelling of **PERVERSION** conveyed a sense of "pleasure and power" for academics studying sexuality and the 'perverts' themselves.

HYPOCRISY as Middle Class society exhibited "blatant and fragmented perversion," readily engaging in perversion but regulating where it could take place. In 18th century Britain 1 in 5 women were prostitutes – Nelson's mistress Emma **HAMILTON** started out as a 'courtesan'.

The mythical idea that previous generations were **REPRESSED** feeds the modern myth that we now live in a 'garden of earthly delights'. (Foucault)

Culture changes by "interconnected mechanisms" and there has been a proliferation of possible sexualities and forms of **DESIRE**, "a deployment quite independent of the law".

Jimmy **SAVILE** sex abuse scandal (2016) and Harvey **WEINSTEIN**'s alleged abuse of power (2017) illustrate Foucault's argument in 1964 A History of Sexuality, as Foucault argues that power relations define how we see sex and sexuality – the powerful **SUBJUGATE** the weak and convince them of the benefits of compliance (the silence of Weinstein's victims is bought by money, jobs or intimidation).

Roger **SCRUTON** (Sexual Desire, 1986) rejects Foucault's claim that sexual morality is culturally **RELATIVE** and criticises Foucault for assuming that there could be societies in which a "problematisation" of the sexual did not occur.

"No history of thought could show the 'problematisation' of sexual experience to be peculiar to certain specific social formations: it is characteristic of personal experience generally, and therefore of every genuine social order". Roger Scruton, Sexual Desire

The fact that Leviticus chapter 18 defines a **PURITY CODE** which causes to stone to death adulterous women and homosexuals as evil doesn't mean that we don't have our own purity code (for example, found in the extreme disgust of paedophilia – a view different from the Greeks).

Gender as a Fluid Concept – Judith Butler (Gender Trouble 1990)

Christianity has encouraged society to impose a **BINARY** (two-sided) relation of women and men. This is then **IDEALISED** as a **HETEROSEXUA**L form, and in the ideal of a two parent family.

Feminists reject the idea that **BIOLOGY** is **DESTINY** (link this to the **TELEOLOGICAL** view of human identity in Natural Law) , but then develop an account of patriarchal culture which assumed that masculine and feminine genders would inevitably be built up from 'male' and 'female' bodies, making the same destiny just as inescapable.

Butler (1956-) argues (with Simone de Beauvoir) that gender is a **SOCIAL CONSTRUCT**. The idea is not fixed, but fluid. Gender is created by repetition of a type of **BODY LANGUAGE** and social attitudes to rebellion (such as disgust at cross-dressing). With Foucault she sees sex (male, female) as causing gender **STEREOTYPES** (masculine, feminine) which is seen to cause desire (towards the other gender).

'There is no gender identity behind the expressions of gender; ... identity is performatively constituted by the very "expressions" that are said to be its results.' (Judith Butler, Gender Trouble, p. 25)

PERFORMATIVITY of gender is a stylised repetition of acts, an imitation or miming of the dominant **CONVENTIONS** of gender. "The act that one does, the act that one performs is, in a sense, an act that's been going on before one arrived on the scene" (Gender Trouble).

"Gender is an impersonation and becoming gendered involves impersonating an ideal that nobody actually inhabits" (Judith Butler, interview with Liz Kotz in Artforum).

"Performativity has to do with **REPETITION**, very often the repetition of oppressive and painful gender norms" (Judith Butler, Gender Trouble).

Butler calls for **SUBVERSIVE ACTION** in the present: 'gender trouble' -- the mobilisation, subversive confusion, and proliferation of genders -- and therefore identity. She would approve of the transgender movement and its forms of direct action and protest in the UK.

Gender and Women's Liberation

PARADOX in a world of liberation and increased rights we still have the silence surrounding Savile and Weinstein, incidence of domestic and other violence against women, and the continued inequalities in pay and promotion in the workplace. Key dates include:

- **1885** Married women could keep hold of their wealth which previously passed to the husband, so restricting divorce.

- **1864** Contagious Diseases Act reacts to prevalence of venereal disease amongst the armed forces (30%) by permitting "policeman to arrest prostitutes in ports and army towns and bring them in to have compulsory checks for venereal disease. If the women were suffering from sexually transmitted diseases they were placed in a locked hospital until cured". **JOSEPHINE BUTLER** launches protest movement at the labelling and degrading of women.

- **1914-18** Women occupy many men's jobs in armaments factories, but in 1918 Unions insist they are made redundant to make way for returning men.

- **1918** Women over 30 obtain the vote after eight year suffragette struggle.

- **1928** Women over 21 obtain the vote.

- **1960s** the Pill allows women to regulate fertility, (Queen Victoria had eight children) experienced by both upper and lower classes.

- **1967** Abortion Reform Act allows termination up to 28 weeks if certain criteria fulfilled. Mental health criterion easily the most popular.

- **1969** Divorce Reform Act allows divorce for 'irretrievable breakdown' rather than just proof of adultery.

- **2004** Gender Recognition Act allows you to apply for a Gender recognition Certificate and so legally change gender after psychiatric assessment for gender dysphoria.

- **2014** Gay couples can be legally married (but not in church).

- **2017** Church of England issues transgender guidance for its 4,700 schools - "pupils need to be able to play with the many cloaks of identity' and should be able 'to explore the many possibilities of who they might be" including gay, lesbian and transgender. "Transphobic bullying causes damage and leads to mental health disorders", Archbishop of Canterbury.

- **2017** a A Bill to make gender identity a protected characteristic under the Equality Act 2010 in place of gender reassignment and to make associated provision for transgender and other persons halted due to the election.

The Changing idea of Family

Comparing 2005 and 2015, we see a snapshot of a profound change in the concept of family continuing (from nuclear to reconstituted, and from **EXTENDED** to nuclear, and from two parent to one parent and from married to cohabiting).

You don't need to learn detailed statistics for A level.

However it may be worth knowing that the fastest growth has been in **COHABITING** couples followed by **LONE PARENT** families in the decade 2005-15. Married and civil partner families have not grown significantly in the ten year period. However, they are still the largest group overall at 8/19 million (42%). Only around a third of households have two people in them.

So we can say with confidence – families are much less likely to be presided over by a married couple than they were forty years ago – family life is far more **FRAGMENTED** and disparate (lone parent, reconstituted, gay or cohabiting, rather than married). Moreover there are many people of any gender living alone. There may be psychological and social **CONSEQUENCES** of these changes.

From **2014** gay people can legally marry (2% of total) – but overwhelmingly in non-religious services (gay couples can't get married in Church by church law).

Christian views on Gender Roles

Augustine on Gender Roles

In Confessions Augustine list of the qualities of his mother Monica - patience, mildness, obedience, selfless service of others, temperance, piety, and even an aversion to gossip, are **STEREOTYPICAL** feminine virtues and vices.

He also describes his long-term relationship with a **CONCUBINE**. Women have one of two roles – mother or lover. Unlike Aquinas, Augustine sees men and women of equal rational capacity , but women by nature submissive because they are **WEAKER**.

Elaine **PAGEL**'s (1989) analyses of the cultural implications of the doctrine of **ORIGINAL SIN** , especially the role of the story of the Fall in Genesis 3. Pagels lays the blame for Christian sexual repression and misogyny (woman hatred) on Augustine, arguing that Augustine's pessimistic views of sexuality, politics, and human nature would come to dominate in Western culture, and that

"Adam, Eve, and the serpent—our ancestral story— would continue, often

in some version of its Augustinian form, to affect our lives to the present day." (Elaine Pagels, Adam, Eve and the Serpent, page 34)

Aquinas on Gender Roles

Aquinas follows **ST PAUL** (*1 Corinthians 11:10 "woman was created for the sake of man"*) in seeing women as **INTELLECTUALLY** inferior. Aquinas sees Ephesians 5:22 "the husband is head of the wife" by virtue of greater intellectual wisdom."Men are wiser and more discerning, and not so quickly taken in", he says.

In attempting to interpret **ARISTOTLE** Aquinas accepts his biological assertion that men are the **ACTIVE AGENT** in reproduction, and women the passive (submissive). It is part of **NATURAL LAW** that women are placed in submission to men – and have to obey men.

Luther (1483-1536) on Gender Roles

The creation of Adam and Eve is God's way of preventing human loneliness (**GENESIS 2**).

Adam and Eve were equals before God, and equally culpable in the **FALL**.

But (like Aquinas) Luther saw men as **SUPERIOR** and more guided by reason and destined to lead in life, and women destined to **SUBMIT.** Women had responsibilities for children and the home. The Lutheran view included equality in principle, but superiority and subordination in practice echoes the contradiction in **ST PAUL** (*Galatians 3:28 'there is neither male nor female'* versus *Ephesians 5:22 "wives submit to your husbands"*).

Luther formulated the doctrine of three estates, which divided society into church, family and state each governed by a **PATRIARCHAL** household as their ideal, i.e. a structure in which the father exercised authority but was also a caring protector. But the **REFORMATION** picture overall is more ambiguous.

MELANCTHON (1497-1560) had theological discussions with highly intelligent women. Luther emphasised that a father performs a Christian act when washing his children's dirty nappies, for example. He also expressed his patriarchal respect for his own wife by calling her Mr Kathy.

Modern church on Gender Roles – Catholic, Liberal Protestant (USA)

The **EPISCOPALIAN** Church of America is the most **LIBERAL** of the Anglican communion of churches. They argue that gender matters because of language, imagery and power relations.

ESCHATOLOGICAL hope is for a future where gender ceases to matter – meantime we make small steps towards **JUSTICE** and **EQUALITY** for women.

"The expression of gender and sexuality are conditioned by culture and by experiences of oppression, especially as racial and ethnic diversity are considered" *(Episcopalian Church, USA)*

The structures of leadership, the language and the practices need to work together to transform the present.

In the Church of England, women priests were first ordained in **1993** and the first woman Bishop, Libby Lane, consecrated in **2015**. Currently there are 12/78 women Bishops (October 2017).

Christian Views on Social Changes

Linda **WOODHEAD** argues that a gap has opened up between Church Teaching and social attitudes on issues such as contraception and gay marriage. The church, faced with the challenge of **RELATIVISM,** has made increasingly tentative steps towards reform – and in the case of the **CATHOLIC** church, has held steadfastly in public to an orthodox (patriarchal) line.

So the increase in UK citizens identifying as **NO RELIGION** (in 2016 51%) does not equate to a lack of **SPIRITUALITY** but a rejection of orthodox forms of Christianity and the embracing of new forms of spirituality (such as New Age, meditation, mindfulness etc).

The Church of England continues to reject gay marriage in church, whilst taking a contradictory view on homosexual sex – gay priests must be celibate (but often in practice are not) whereas church members generally should be encouraged to be faithful to their partner.

In the Catholic church, research suggest only around 11% of Catholic women in the USA follow the prohibition on contraception and abortion, and 31% are on the pill – so fuelling allegations of **DOUBLE STANDARDS**. Meantime, in Africa **AIDS** infection remains endemic and safe sex officially discouraged by the Church.

CATHOLICS FOR CHOICE argues that "Abstinence before marriage and faithfulness in a marriage is beyond the realm of possibility here. The issue is to protect life. That must be our fundamental goal. African people must use condoms."

Christian Teaching – the Bible

Ephesians 5:22-33

EPHESIANS 5 needs to be interpreted in the context of a revolutionary document presented to a patriarchal culture. *"The apostolic letters are addressed to people living in an environment marked by that same traditional way of thinking and acting"*. *"All the reasons in favour of the "subjection" of woman to man in marriage must be understood in the sense of a "mutual subjection" of both "out of reverence for Christ"*. Mulieris Dignitatem p 24

Christian Teaching- Roman Catholic Mulieris Dignitatem (MD)

1971 Pope appoints commission to ensure "effective promotion of the dignity and the responsibility of women" culminates in 1988 in **MULIERIS DIGNITATEM** (of the vocation and dignity of women).

Reaffirms **IDEAL** of Mary as obedient and submissive handmaid of the Lord (Luke1:38), and pure virgin. Like Jesus himself, she is called to **SERVE**. She is the new **EVE** and the prototype of a **NEW CREATION**.

Also confirms the Creation order that "both man and woman are human beings to an equal degree, both are created in God's image". Genesis 1:28

Acknowledges the contradiction between two creation accounts (Genesis 1:28 versus Genesis 2:18-25). MD asserts, against traditional teaching, that

"The biblical text provides sufficient bases for recognising the essential equality of man and woman from the point of view of their humanity".

(Mulieris Dignitatem p14)

Word equality here does not mean 'equal rights' to exercise leadership in the church. Interpretation here is **RELATIONAL** and **TRINITARIAN**.

"Man - whether man or woman - is the only being among the creatures of the visible world that God the Creator "has willed for its own sake"; that creature is thus a person. Being a person means striving towards self-realisation (the Council text speaks of self-discovery), which can only be achieved "through a sincere gift of self". (Mulieris Dignitatem p16)

The model for this interpretation of the person is God himself as **TRINITY** (God in Three Persons) as a communion of Persons. To say that man is created in the **IMAGE** and likeness of God means that man is called to exist "for others, to become a gift", (Mulieris Dignitatem).

Affirms the feminine and masculine qualities of God eg "Can a woman forget her sucking child, that she should have no compassion on the son of her womb? Even these may forget, yet I will not forget you". (Isaiah 49:14-15).

The **FALL** 'obscures' and 'diminishes' the image of God but does not eliminate it. But consequences include pain (for women) and death for all. Man also 'shall have **DOMINION** (power) over women" (Genesis 3:16) as a part of the consequences of sin.

However, all 'unjust situations' should be remedied because the fundamental equality of Genesis 2 overrides the effects of the Fall in Genesis 3.

Gender differences need to be preserved as part of the **NATURAL CREATED ORDER**. even the rightful opposition of women to what is expressed in the biblical words "He shall rule over you" (Genesis 3:16) must not under any condition lead to the "masculinisation" of women. In the name of liberation from male "domination", women must not appropriate to themselves male characteristics contrary to their own feminine "originality".

Despite evidence of a new relationship to women reflected in Jesus actions and teachings, and the presence of women as the first witnesses of resurrection , MD reaffirms that

"Virginity and motherhood are two particular dimensions of the fulfilment of the female personality". (Mulieris Dignitatem p 17).

MARY DALY would see the depiction of women as virgin, mother or whore as part of the conditioning of **PATRIARCHY** whereas **DAPHNE HAMPSON** would see the complex interpretations of Mulieris Dignitatem as part of the **IRREDUCIBLY** patriarchal nature of historical Christianity, the Bible and all its interpretations which justify inequality (such as the Catholic teaching against women priests and bishops).

Possible Exam Questions

1. "Christians should resist current secular views of gender" Discuss

2. Evaluate the view that secular views of gender equality have undermined Christian gender roles

3. "Motherhood liberates rather than restricts". Discuss

4. Critically evaluate the view that idea of family is entirely culturally determined.

5. "Christianity follows where culture leads". Discuss

Key Quotes

"One is not born, but rather one becomes a woman.. it is civilisation that produces this creature." Simone de Beauvoir.

"Gender is an impersonation . . . becoming gendered involves impersonating an ideal that nobody actually inhabits." Judith Butler, Gender Trouble

"My argument for the "moral significance" of gender is an extensive attack on the Kantian assumption behind modern feminism—the assumption that what I am essentially is a person, and that persons are essentially genderless." Roger Scruton, Sexual Desire

"According to Scruton's Aristotelian argument, love is to sexual desire as the mature flourishing life of a tree is to the young developing plant". Martha Nussbaum

"There is no gender identity behind the expressions of gender; ... identity is performatively constituted by the very "expressions" that are said to be its results." Judith Butler, Gender Trouble

"Even a pioneering feminist like Germaine Greer is forbidden to speak on campus lest her belief in real and objective sexual differences should threaten vulnerable students who have yet to decide which gender they are". Independent 3.11.17

"Within Christianity, more than in any other religion, women have had a

special dignity, of which the New Testament shows us many important aspects." Pope Paul VI

Further Reading

Tong, R. (2013) Feminist Thought, Routledge, Chapter 1

McGrath, A. (2010 5th Edition) A Christian Theology, Wiley-Blackwell, pages 88–89, 336–337

More A. Female Sexuality (Routledge, 2005) synopsis available on peped.org

Messer, N. (2006) SCM Study Guide to Christian Ethics, SCM Press, Chapter 8.

Mulieris Dignitatem, Roman Catholic Encyclical available on peped.org

Pagels, E. Adam, Eve and The Serpent (Vintage, 1989)

Ephesians 5:22–33 peped.org > Philosophy > christian-thought > feminism

Gender and Theology

Background

Paradoxically, Christianity presents itself as a prophetic movement of liberation and belief in a **NEW HEAVEN** and a **NEW EARTH** redeemed by the faithful. Mary **DALY** and Daphne **HAMPSON** are post-Christians feminists who reject the very basis of Christianity and the Christian God-concept. Rosemary **RUETHER** remains a Catholic calling the church to repent and change.

A word of warning though: Christianity isn't one entity and it is dangerous to **GENERALISE**. The **MONTANISTS** of the second to sixth century had women leaders and prophets, and the **QUAKERS** of the past 400 years have always followed a priestless equality where anyone can speak a word from God. Perhaps Christianity (following Emporer **CONSTANTINE**'s conversion in 316) have become too enmeshed in the power structures of many societies to be a prophetic movement and has become a rather laggardly reflection of its times.

Specification

A level requires that we study Ruether's discussion of the maleness of Christ and its implications for salvation including:

- Jesus' challenge to the male **WARRIOR MESSIAH** expectation

- God as the female **WISDOM** principle

- Jesus as the **INCARNATION** of wisdom

Daly's claim that *'if God is male then the male is God' (1996:76)* and its implications for Christianity, including:

- Christianity's 'Unholy Trinity' of rape, genocide and war
  - spirituality experienced through nature

Key terms

- **APOCRYPHA:** That part of the Bible rejected by Protestant Christianity, but containing Wisdom literature which exalts the feminine.

- **ESCHATOLOGY:** The end times, traditionally a time in the future when God judges the world. In feminism, eschatology is realized now with judgement on patriarchy and formation of a new society.

- **FEMINISM:** A movement campaigning for the rights, empowerment and equality of women.

- **GENOCIDE:** The attempt to eliminate a race or a religious group by extreme violence and murder

- **GOD/ESS:** Ruether's genderless term for God

- **HERMENEUTICS:** The study of methods of interpretation and the textual generation of meaning

- **INCARNATION:** Embodiment of some value of goodness or aspect of God

- **MESSIAH:** The 'anointed one' sent by God in fulfilment of Old Testament prophecy to liberate and redeem Israel

- **MONTANISM:** prophetic movement in the second century where women prophesied and claimed visions directly from Christ.

- **PATRIARCHY:** (Two Latin words, pater/arche) rule of the male. A form of society where men dominate, denigrate and oppress women.

- **SEXISM:** Prejudice, stereotyping, or discrimination, typically against women, on the basis of sex.

- **SHEKINAH:** The glory of God which traditionally shone forth from the altar, expelled by patriarchy and rediscovered in the Exodus community of women.

- **SPIRITUALITY:** Response to the metaphysical reality beyond the physical, where the individual forms patterns of self-determination that build the common good.

Structure of Thought - Ruether

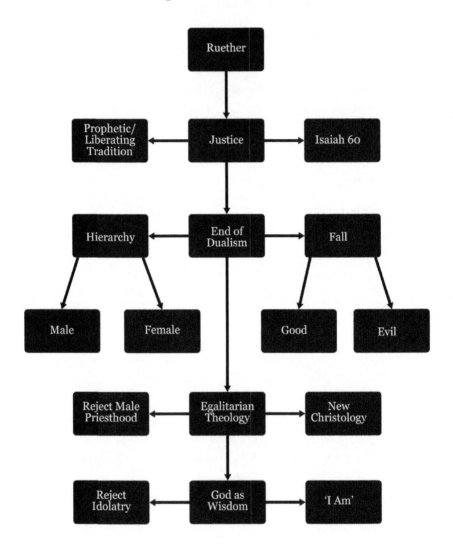

Hermeneutics of Suspicion

Paul **RICOEUR** (1913-2005) asks us to adopt a **HERMENEUTIC OF SUSPICION** when reading a text such as the Bible. We need to be suspicious of the **MOTIVES**, the **VALUES**, the culture of those who wrote it, and not just project our own values onto the text. James O'Donnell comments

"Liberation means, therefore, to opt for the exercise of an ideological suspicion in order to unmask the unconscious ideological structures which dominate and which favour a powerful, privileged minority." (O'Donnell 1982:32)

There is a **WORLD BEHIND** the text (the culture of Jesus' day) and there is a world **IN FRONT** of the text, our own culture. These **TWO HORIZONS** (Gadamer's term) need to merge in a valid interpretation that is **CRITICAL**.

Elizabeth Schüssler **FIORENZA** argues that theology is the product of each writer's experience and that this is determined by the historical and **SOCIAL CONTEXT** of every theologian. Theology is culturally conditioned and shapes, reflects, and serves a particular group's or individual's interests, (Fiorenza 1975:616).

Ruether argues that the Bible is riddled with **PATRIARCHY** and emerged from a world of hierarchy with males in charge. The **FEMININE** is constructed from these patriarchal values.

The social relationships are **ARCHAIC** and inappropriate for our time: they are reflected in a male clergy and a continued tolerance of **INJUSTICE** and **INEQUALITY**.

Behind the interpretation of the Bible lies the acceptance of **ARISTOTLE**'s biology that sees men and women as two separate classes of human and whereby

"The female is not only secondary to the male but lacks full human status in physical strength, moral self-control, and mental capacity. The lesser "nature" thus confirms the female's subjugation to the male as her "natural" place in the universe". (Ruether 1985:65)

Ruether's Hermeneutic

Controlling principle – whatever denigrates women is rejected, whatever builds up and values women is accepted. Then it is **EXPERIENCE** (rather than history) which is the starting-point of theology. The Bible needs to be interpreted anew, and the story of **REDEMPTION** retold in the light of women's experience. This may be linked to the **EXISTENTIAL** theology of Paul **TILLICH**.

There is a **PROPHETIC PRINCIPLE** in the Bible which can be rediscovered and brought to the fore: emphasising **JUSTICE** and the call to be a new people of **LIBERATION. ISAIAH 60** gives a radical vision of a just world order.

"God's Shekinah, Holy Wisdom, the Mother-face of God has fled from the high thrones of patriarchy and has gone into exodus with us". Ruether, 1985:87

The counter-culture of early Christianity which emphasised this were suppressed, for example, the female **PROPHETS** Priscilla and Maximilla in **MONTANISM.** Priscilla claimed a night vision in which Christ slept by her side "in the form of woman, clad in a bright garment". She adopted a priestly ministry with direct voices and visions from God. Montanists were persecuted and ultimately suppressed with violence in the sixth century.

SEXISM is a sin against God/ess and against the fundamental golden thread of **JUSTICE** within the Bible.

"The dominant Christian tradition, if corrected by feminism, offers viable categories for interpreting human existence and building redemptive communities" Ruether, 1985:123

Ruether's God-Concept

GOD/ESS is the ground of all being. God is **GENDERLESS** and to turn God into the **MALE** is a form of **IDOLATRY** that serves men's interests.

In the **OLD TESTAMENT**, **YAHWEH** is the name of God – it means 'no name' or I **AM WHO I AM**.

Patriarchy encourages **HIERARCHY** with the idea of **TRANSCENDENCE**. Ruether emphasises **IMMANENCE** – God as **BEING** within all things.

Ruether sees God as **WISDOM** – the Greek word **LOGOS** and the idea in **WISDOM** literature (the Book of Wisdom is part of the **APOCRYPHA** – not in the Protestant Bible). **GOD/ESS** has sources in **PAGANISM**, and Babylonian **CREATION** myths – but the **MOTHER NATURE** idea was suppressed by the early Church.

LANGUAGE reflects patriarchal values – **FATHER**, Lord, King. "**OUR FATHER...THY KINGDOM COME**".

Can a Male Saviour Save?

Jesus' **GENDER** is irrelevant. Maleness of Christ has no **THEOLOGICAL** significance. The **MESSIAH** is an iconoclastic (idol-smashing) **PROPHET** in the tradition of **ISAIAH** or **AMOS**.

The real Jesus needs to be rediscovered and the Church should **REPENT** and cast off patriarchal values and images. Jesus is the **INCARNATE WISDOM** of God (**LOGOS**, John 1).

Such a rediscovery embraces a new relation to the earth (link with Mary Daly's **GYN/ECOLOGY**). Feminism is, says Daly, **BIOPHILIC** (loves life). This creative thinking creates communities of liberation who engage in play of ideas. Ruether agrees.

The New Age and the Eschatological Community

Does not lie in the future, **ESCHATOLOGICALLY** as in patriarchal ideas – beyond the grave. Link with theological **IMMANENCE** (God is here now, the new community is realised here, now)

It is brought into being now in the **REDEEMED COMMUNITY – REALISED ESCHATOLOGY**.

Ruether believes church can be redeemed by forming new **BASE COMMUNITIES** with **JUSTICE** at their heart. **CLERICALISM** (male priesthood) is a product of patriarchy and should be rejected.

Early Church experiments such as **MONTANISM** (2nd century) had women leaders: in Acts there is a prophetess, and Paul's argument "I do not allow women to have authority in the Church" (1 Corinthians) only makes sense in context of the rise of women **PROPHETS** in Corinth and discord that surrounded it.

Criticisms of Ruether

In a 1986 debate, Daphne Hampson makes three criticisms of Ruether's position (acronym **HIS**).

- **Historical** Roots of Christianity are Sexist. Ruether ignores the historically-entrenched nature of Christianity, which 'necessarily has one foot in the past'. Incarnation means that God became a human being at a particular time, within a patriarchal worldview. That Jesus only chose male apostles may be no accident. Hampson concludes that 'it cannot be the case that God is related in a particular way to a certain history'. Like Daly, Hampson is a post-Christian. Anthony Thiselton agrees:

"Some texts, by their very nature, draw part of their meaning from the actions, history and life with which they are inextricably interwoven"; Thiselton, New Horizons pg 66.

- **Incarnational** Doctrine is sexist. God 'sent his son'. Metaphors for God are male (with a few exceptions that are never developed). God calls Jesus 'My Beloved Son, whom I have chosen,' and asks Jesus' followers to 'listen to him' (Luke 9:35). Christian creeds ask us to affirm belief in "Jesus Christ, his only Son, our Lord'. Lord and Son are both patriarchal images.

- **Symbolic** world is sexist. The revelation of Christ in history is full of patriarchal symbols and messages. The Prodigal Son is having property divided between two men (Luke 15:11-35). The Good Samaritan is a male. When Jesus visits Martha and Mary, Mary is busy cooking and Martha commended for sitting passively at Jesus' feet, (Luke 1:38-42). Women who were Resurrection witnesses were not believed because the testimony of women is unreliable. Moreover, Paul is a Rabbi and retains some of the Levitical symbolic world of Rabbinic Judaism. Hampson points out 'we do not have stories of a man sitting at the feet of a female teacher'. When stories circulate in Corinth of women prophets, Paul seeks to suppress the upsurge by writing two letters to the Corinthians, both against women's liberation, insisting 'women keep silent in church' (1 Corinthians 14:34-5).

Hampson therefore accuses Ruether of misrepresenting the profoundly historical nature of Christian patriarchy, which still affects Christian theology and practice. Hampson is a **POST-CHRISTIAN**, Ruether a Christian **LIBERATION** theologian.

Background - Mary Daly

Mary Daly (1928-2010) was a radical lesbian feminist theologian who taught at **BOSTON COLLEGE**. She almost always refused to let men into her classes, in 1999, a male student sued the school for discrimination. Daly was suspended and ultimately refused to comply. She also stated she found men disruptive. Lawrence Cunningham calls her 'the gold standard of **ABSOLUTE FEMINISM**."

Structure of Thought - Mary Daly

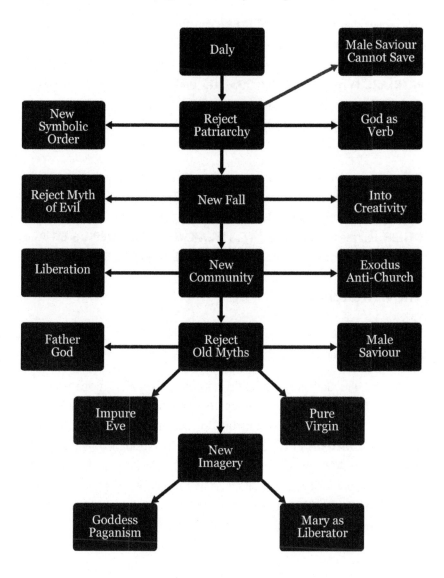

The Myths that Bolster Patriarchy

Daly argues that male **MYTH-MAKERS** constructed an image of the feminine to mould women for their own purposes. The male is the **ROBBER** who robs women of "their myths, their energy, their divinity, their very selves". **PATRIARCHY** has 'stolen our **COSMOS** and turned it into Cosmopolitan magazine" and is the prevailing religion of the entire planet, whose essential message is **NECROPHILIA** (love of **DEATH** eg crucifixion and **MORTIFICATION** - putting our sins to death by self-flagellation).

She calls women to have the courage 'to see and to be' and represent the greatest challenge to the religions of the world. The ultimate **SIN** is patriarchal religion; yet women are **COMPLICIT** by living out the role of the submissive **OTHER**, represented in Christianity as **WEAK, OBEDIENT, DEPRAVED**. As in **AQUINAS'** thought, men are **SUPERIOR, WISE, STRONG, RATIONAL**.

The Patriarchal God

The language of the **FATHER** God legitimates male supremacy and oppression of women – "as God is male the male becomes god".

She rejects the God-image of Christianity in favour of participation in an **ULTIMATE REALITY** - a God-concept 'beyond and beneath'. The **IMAGE** of **GOD** is the creative potential in all human beings. In this **TRANSFORMATION** of symbols of God, God is transformed from a **NOUN** (**FATHER, LORD**) to a verb who is "form-destroying, form-creating, transforming power that makes all things new" (Daly, Beyond God the Father). God is **BEING** and **BECOMING**. We might describe this as a rejection of the Christian God and a rediscovery of earlier feminine god-concepts.

Myth of the Feminine

Daly accuses **AUGUSTINE** and **AQUINAS** of misogyny (women hatred) as they deny women the power to reach their full potential.

The male constructs the feminine as the originator of **EVIL** in the myth of the **FALL** and its interpretations. **EVE** is represented as the **SCAPEGOAT** of male sexual guilt. Daly encourages women to enter a new Fall - a **FALL** into **FREEDOM**, involving eating the forbidden fruit of **WISDOM** all over again. Two images of women: the **VIRGIN** and the **WHORE**, represented in the image of the **PURE VIRGIN MARY** and the fallen **MARY MAGDALENE**.

• **MARY** = the impossible virgin (still submissive to the will of the Father-God)

• **MARY MAGDALENE** (the fallen woman) = all other women cast in the image of the fallen **EVE**.

Daly calls women to stop playing the role of meek, subservient 'complement' to men, to re-imagine their power and renew the world.

Yet the virgin **MARY** can be adopted by feminism as a symbol of the **AUTONOMOUS** woman, the first woman to fall into **PARADISE**. Mary echoes back to a pre-Christian era of the **GREAT GODDESS**.

The Scapegoat Christ

Daly believes Jesus was simply a limited human being. It is **IDOLATRY** to suggest a **MALE** saviour can represent the eternal **BEING** which is God. Jesus is portrayed by patriarchy as the **SCAPEGOAT** for the sins originating in **EVE**, and the twin idealisations of **CHRIST** and **MARY** have nothing to do with history.

The projection of our evil onto these twin figures of **PURITY** results from an **INABILITY** to accept our own guilt. Feminism rejects the **SCAPEGOAT** Christ with its projections of **VICTIMHOOD** and the worship of the violence of the **CROSS** as part of the **NECROPHILIA** (love of **DEATH**) of patriarchy.

In the development of patriarchy, the male priest becomes the sole mediator controlling access to the deity. Women need to affirm **BIOPHILIA** (love of life).

A Fall into the Sacred

Women in exercising their **FREEDOM** and **POWER** fall into a new sacred space, a **SECOND COMING**, escaping the false **PARADISE** of patriarchal enslavement. They practise **BECOMING** by renouncing the traditional dichotomy of **HETEROSEXUAL/HOMOSEXUAL**, which are patriarchal classifications, to live in an environment that is "beyond, beneath and all around".

Women empowered cut loose from the **PSYCHOSEXUAL** chains that bind them to a patriarchal set of images, and a patriarchal power structure. Women are by nature **ANTI-CHURCH** with its over-emphasis on sexual and gender differences. Women have to 'live now the freedom we are fighting for', and **FEAR** and **GUILT** are no longer used as weapons of oppression. She calls both men and women to leave the church and become "an **EXODUS** community prepared to get on with the business of **LIVING**". Indeed men may understand the manipulation of **POWER** better as they see it from **WITHIN**.

"Male religion entombs women in sepulchres of silence in order to chant its own eternal and dreary dirge to a past that never was". Mary Daly, Beyond God the Father, page 145

Ultimately Daly believes in a new **COSMIC COVENANT** – which renounces the old order of meaningless desires, violence and war.

Gyn/Ecology

Daly plays on words to encourage women to 'weave tapestries of our own kind". She rages against the oppressive system in which "patriarchy is the homeland of males" and where they oppress and demonise women in rites of **SUTTEE** or **WITCH-BURNING**.

She analyses the **LANGUAGE** of patriarchy and the mind/body/spirit **POLLUTION** this has brought about. **PHALLIC** myths predominate – from the Coca-Cola advert for the **REAL THING** to the Christian hymns glorying in the **DEATH** and real presence of Christ. With spiritual pollution comes pollution of the planet – as the male 'threatens to **TERMINATE** life on the planet through rape (of nature), genocide and war'.

"If life is to survive on this planet, there must be a decontamination of the Earth. I think this will be accompanied by an evolutionary process that will result in a drastic reduction of the population of males." (Gyn/Ecology page 54)

To escape the enslavement and **DENIGRATION** of the male, women need to invent a **NEW LANGUAGE** and set of social relations. Using **CREATIVE ANGER** and **BRILLIANT BRAVERY**, women rediscover 'our **WOMEN-LOVING** love". "We find our original Being and we SPIN our original **INTEGRITY**" and so put **POWER** and **JOY** back into living.

On contraception she comments, showing her playful use of language:

"It is obvious to Hags that few gynaecologists recommend to their heterosexual patients the most foolproof of solutions, namely Misterectomy.

The Spinsters who propose this way by our be-ing, liv-ing, speak-ing can do so with power precisely because we are not preoccupied with ways to get off the heterosexually defined contraceptive dilemma. " (Gyn/Ecology p.239)

Criticisms of Daly

- Black theologian Audre **LOURDE** criticised Daly for refusing to acknowledge the '**HERSTORY** and myth' of women of colour. The severe oppression they have suffered greatly outweighs the discrimination of white women. There's a racial bias to Daly's work and a racist indifference to the plight of minorities who suffer greatest oppression.

- Patriarchy cannot assist in explaining why only a few men in a patriarchy use violence against women and why many males have campaigned for women's rights over the centuries (the first man being Jesus himself who overthrew aspects of anti-women purity code of **LEVITICUS**).

- Daly wanted **WOMEN** to rule men and was herself a lesbian and vegetarian. "I really don't care about men" she commented in an interview. Yet isn't this perpetuating the **DUALISM** she herself rejects as oppressive?

- The **FRAMEWORK** of Patriarchy is assumed in all instances. There is no other explanation given for witch-burning (Christian) or suttee (Hindu). Paradoxically, Enlightenment enquiry provoked an upsurge of interest in alchemy and other forms of magic: it is arguably the flip-side of the stress on autonomous reason. James I wrote a book on witches.

- People who criticise her she calls "**FEMBOTS** doing Daddy's work".

- No analysis of class, wealth or race as instruments of oppression of women.

Confusions to Avoid

1. **Feminists cannot be Christians**. Feminists like Ruether argue that Christianity can be restored to a lost **PROPHETIC** movement, transforming society, but only if patriarchy is rejected. A male saviour is irrelevant to salvation and the male perspective is a gloss overlaying the true gospel, which can be reconstructed as a gospel of liberation and hope. However, both Daphne Hampson and Mary Daly call women out of the church and see Christianity as irredeemably patriarchal. They are post-Christian feminists.

2. **The Church has no response to feminism**. This isn't a fair assessment because the Protestant churches have reformed themselves and allowed women priests and bishops (where appropriate to their order of ministry). The Church of England ordained women **PRIESTS** in 1993 and women **BISHOPS** in 2013. The Roman Catholic Church produced a brave apologetic for its position in not allowing women priests and bishops in Mulieris Dignitatem, which lay great emphasis on the equality of the sexes, but failed to reconcile the **CONTRADICTION** in the Bible between the Paul of Galatians (there is neither male nor female) and the Paul of Ephesians and Corinthians (wives obey your husbands, and "I do not allow women to have authority over a man'). Moreover, the Catholic persistence in advocating the **RHYTHM** method of contraception suggests that the **AUTONOMY** of women and their right to choose is still being overridden by the male perspective.

3. **A male saviour cannot save**. This extreme position, taken by Mary Daly, would appear to overlook the revolutionary attitude of Jesus towards women whom he included in his inner circle and addressed as equals – "daughter, your faith has made you well, go in peace" (Mark 5). Arguably when Jesus 'emptied himself taking the form of a servant' (Philippians 2:7), he also gave up the genderless **INFINITY** of God (Yahweh – means 'I am who I am'). God cannot have a gender and so if Jesus is one with God his gender must be irrelevant for salvation. Messiah is a genderless idea. Emphasis on the gender of Christ and the virginity of Mary comes later as the male-dominated church hierarchy produces creeds which impose uniformity on belief and cast out so-called heretics, such as the **MONTANISTS**.

Possible Exam Questions

1. 'A male saviour cannot save'. Discuss with reference to the theologies of Rosemary Ruether and Mary Daly.

2. "If God is male the male is God'. Discuss

3. Critically contrast the theologies of Ruether and Daly.

4. "The Church is irrevocably patriarchal'. Discuss

5. "God is genderless, and so the idea of the Father-God is idolatry". Discuss

6. "Only a spirituality of women can save the planet from environmental degradation and war'. Discuss

Key Quotes

"If God is male then the male is God' Mary Daly (1996:76)

"It is obvious to Hags that few gynaecologists recommend to their heterosexual patients the most foolproof of solutions, namely Misterectomy". Mary Daly (Gyn/Ecology p239)

"The dominant Christian tradition, if corrected by feminism, offers viable categories for interpreting human existence and building redemptive communities". Rosemary Ruether, 1985:123

"Some texts, by their very nature, draw part of their meaning from the actions, history and life with which they are inextricably interwoven". Anthony Thiselton, New Horizons pg 66.

"The female is not only secondary to the male but lacks full human status in physical strength, moral self-control, and mental capacity. The lesser "nature" thus confirms the female's subjugation to the male as her "natural" place in the universe". Rosemary Ruether (1985:65)

Reading

Listen to Mary Daly interview
https://archive.org/details/KDVS_The_Fringe_4-5-06

Mary Daly, Beyond God the Father, (Beacon, 1992)

Mary Daly, Can a Male Saviour Save? (Select 'Extracts' from:
http://peped.org/philosophicalinvestigations/christian-thought/feminism/)

Elisabeth Schussler Fiorenza, Sharing Her Word (T & T Clarke, 1998)

Daphne Hampson, After Christianity (SCM, 2002)

Rosemary Ruether, Sexism and God-talk (Beacon, 1993)

Bible Passages such as 2 Corinthians 11:3 and 1 Tim 2:14 became the argument for the subordination of women, and Mark 5 and John 8 for Jesus' more liberating attitudes to women. Isaiah 60 gives the prophetic call for justice. Paul in Galatians 3:16 seems to contradict Ephesians 5. Can they be reconciled?

Hampson, (After Christianity, 2002), states that if Christianity is true, God cannot be thought of as moral or good "given the harm that this myth has done to women" (Hampson 2002: xv). The Christian myth is misogynistic (Hampson 2002: xvi) and morally suspect (Hampson 2002: vxiii).

Exam Rescue Remedy

Introductions should include:

1. **Definition** of terms: Identification of the theories/arguments referred to the title and any **TECHNICAL** vocabulary.

2. **Identification** of the parameters of the question: what are the two opposing perspectives? Remember to discuss **NON-TECHNICAL** vocabulary as well such as 'is stronger than', 'is more effective', 'is meaningless'.

3. **Thesis statement**: Where do you stand in the argument? **IMPOSE** your own line of analysis on the question.

You should plan **SIX** paragraphs including:

1. **Title**: **DISCUSS** the arguments referred to in the title.

2. **Challenge 1**: **DISCUSS** the weaknesses or against the arguments of paragraph 1.

3. **Response 1**: Respond to the weaknesses and challenges discussed in paragraph 2. Summarise or omit if the thesis statement agrees with paragraph 1.

4. **Alternative**: Discuss an alternative/opposing perspective to the arguments of paragraph 1.

5. **Challenge 2**: Discuss the weaknesses or against the arguments of paragraph 4.

6. **Response 2**: Respond to the weaknesses and challenges discussed in paragraph 5. Summarise or omit if the thesis statement disagrees with paragraph 1.

Each paragraph should include:

1. **Hook**: What will this paragraph be about? What scholar/work? Why is this relevant?

2. **Assertions**: What are the attitudes/beliefs/teachings that the scholars present?

3. **Analysis**: How do these assertions work? Why are they presented? How do they form an argument? Use link words and phrases to justify, develop and evaluate.

4. **Justification**: What examples/quotes defend and justify the assertions made?

5. **Link**: How does this paragraph answer the question? How does it link to your thesis statement?

Conclusions should include:

1. **For**: Summarise the arguments for one side of the question.

2. **Against**: Summarise the arguments for the alternative side of the question.

3. **Evaluation**: Evaluate the perspectives and justify the thesis statement.

Revision Access

Opening March 25th 2018

Our unique guides provide you with a special benefit - your own revision site which is fully integrated with the guides and only available to purchasers.

All our revision materials for Christian Thought, Ethics, and Philosophy of Religion are available to each purchaser of any individual or combined peped guide. Resources include model essay samples of questions found at the back of each chapter, and also:

- Articles

- Extracts

- Handouts

- Roadmap

- Summary

- Videos

- Whizz Through Powerpoints

Visit: peped.org/revision-access

Postscript

Andrew Capone is the Head of Religious Education at St Simon Stock Catholic School, Maidstone. He has a Masters of Arts in Classical History and a Joint Bachelors of Arts in Philosophy and Religious Studies. He also offers personal tuition, analytical marking and consultation to Religious Education and Philosophy teachers.

Peter Baron read Politics, Philosophy and Economics at New College, Oxford and afterwards obtained an MLitt for a research degree in Hermeneutics at Newcastle University. He qualified as an Economics teacher in 1982, and taught at Tonbridge School, Kent from 1982-1991. He was ordained as a Church of England priest in 1993, and served in various parishes from 1993-2004. After a period teaching in Italy, he taught Religious Studies at Wells Cathedral School in Somerset from 2006-2012. He is currently a freelance writer, speaker and Managing Editor of Peped. He has authored ten books.

Daniella Dunsmore trained in Theology at Cambridge University. She is currently subject leader in Religious Studies at Thetford Grammar School, speaks at Conferences, and is a Teach First Ambassador.

Printed in Great Britain
by Amazon

37985600R00129